JOHANN JOSEPH FUX, Austrian composer and theorist, was born in 1660 and died in Vienna in 1741. In 1698 he became court composer; in 1704 he was made Kapellmeister at St. Stephen's and eventually Kapellmeister to the court. In this highest of musical posts he served three successive emperors. Among his numerous musical compositions are operas, oratorios, sacred works, and instrumental pieces. His most enduring work is his treatise on counterpoint, *Gradus ad Parnassum.*

The Study of Counterpoint

from JOHANN JOSEPH FUX'S

Gradus ad Parnassum

REVISED EDITION

TRANSLATED AND EDITED BY
ALFRED MANN

WITH THE COLLABORATION OF
JOHN EDMUNDS

W · W · NORTON & COMPANY

New York · London

FIRST PUBLISHED IN THE NORTON LIBRARY 1965

Previously published under the title *Steps to Parnassus. The Study of Counterpoint.*

W. W. Norton & Company, Inc.
500 Fifth Avenue, New York, N.Y. 10110
www.wwnorton.com

W. W. Norton & Company Ltd.
15 Carlisle Street, London W1D 3BS

ISBN-13: 978-0-393-00277-5
ISBN-10: 0-393-00277-2

PRINTED IN THE UNITED STATES OF AMERICA

45th Printing

Contents

The Dialogue

First Part

Second Part

Third Part

Contents

Introduction

The Study of Counterpoint might be compared to the study of perspective. Both were important developments in Renaissance art. Both reflect the rise of three-dimensional thought.

The medieval composer dealt with different voices of a motet in much the way in which the medieval painter portrayed different levels of a landscape. The composition, in both cases, was an aggregate of parts rather than an entity conceived in depth. It is characteristic of medieval music that theorists speak of *discantus*—two-fold melody—even when they refer to a setting of more than two parts. Theirs was a two-dimensional approach to polyphony. The term discantus was the predecessor of the term counterpoint. Early in its use, discantus had acquired the connotation of part-writing that left no room for improvisational freedom but whose rhythm was strictly measured note against note: *punctus contra punctum*.

The word *contrapunctus* emerged about 1300 in a number of tracts the origins of which have not been fully clarified. A first *Introduction to Counterpoint* was for a long time attributed to Johannes de Garlandia, but his authorship—confusing in itself because of the existence of an earlier theorist by the same name—has been questioned by recent scholarship. Doubt has arisen also about the attribution to Johannes de Muris of a treatise dealing with the *Art of Counterpoint* and to Philippe de Vitry, famous master of the *ars nova*, of a similar work. As the involvement of the latter name suggests, however, we can identify the early writers on counterpoint by generation, if not by name; they are representatives of a "New Art," the art of fourteenth-century polyphony. Soon after the term contrapunctus appeared, its application seems to have been extended beyond the strict original meaning, and in a *Treatise of Counterpoint* (1412), the Italian theorist Prosdocimus de Beldemandis pointed out that the contrapuntist had actually become concerned with the problem of *cantus contra cantum*—the problem of judging one complete melody against another rather than note against note.

This realization called for an integration of vertical and horizontal concepts. The phenomenon of counterpoint was gradually recognized in its full complexity. With the fifteenth century began the golden age of polyphony, and the great works of the Burgundian and Flemish masters were followed by theoretical writings commensurate with the noble music of their time. The Flemish writer Johannes Tinctoris, known to music students as the author of the first published dictionary of musical terms, is also the first to discuss systematically the principles of both placing note against note and placing one note against two or more notes. The first species he calls simple counterpoint "based on the proportion of equality, without benefit of the flower of diversity." The second species he calls diminished (i.e. dissolved) or florid counterpoint and declares it superior to the first, saying that "the variety of proportions produces the most agreeable counterpoint, just as the diversity of flowers produces the most beautiful fields." He takes into account the crucial fact that the composer's judgment must be based not only on what he hears at a given moment but what he must keep in mind in the continuity of hearing. He deals extensively with progressions and with comparisons of different passages following one another in a contrapuntal fabric. It is significant that in explaining the word counterpoint itself, he treats "point" no longer as a mere synonym for "note." When he speaks of measurement from point to point, he quite obviously has in mind an analogy with mathematical concepts, and his formulation suggests indeed the imagination and draftsmanship of the masters of optical perspective. Equally apparent in his comprehension of polyphony and his penchant for focused terminology, his strength of perception suggests the advances made into other new territory at the time; his accomplishment stands apart from the writing of earlier theorists as does the global quest of Columbus from the continental expeditions of earlier explorers.

The conquest of a vantage point from which to subject music to the laws of proportion and correlation seems evident also in a new awareness of the distance of time. Tinctoris had drawn a clearer line than writers before him between the past and his own age, and the works of Gioseffo Zarlino, a contemporary of Palestrina and the most eminent of Renaissance theorists, are devoted primarily to summing up the achievements of his age, to reviewing and clarifying a music theory that had become independent of the Middle Ages. In doing so, Zarlino arrived at conclusions that greatly widened the scope of contrapuntal theory, for the term counterpoint is applied in his text to the process of relating one "point" of a composition to another thematically. The word *contrapuntizare*, which Zarlino introduced for this manner of envisioning "the whole composition at once," corresponds to the word "pointing" used subsequently by English theorists for the thematic correlation of various voices within a contrapuntal work.

The perspective of time becomes even more obvious in the attitude of seventeenth-century theory, which began to identify counterpoint with a *stile antico*. Claudio Monteverdi, genius of a revolutionary era in music, raised a fundamental issue by drawing the distinction between a "first practice" and a "second practice" of composition. Entangled in the polemic writing his artistic activity had evoked and in which he had been charged with violating the rules of counterpoint, he boldly asserted that the departures from the acknowledged style constituted a style in themselves and that there was a "practice other than that taught by Zarlino." Thus Monteverdi gave to the music theory of his time a two-fold challenge: to formulate the theoretical basis for a new practice and to

X

re-formulate that of the old. Neither task was completed during the seventeenth century. One called for the establishment of a modern theoretical system not fully realized until the writings of Jean Philippe Rameau, whose new interpretation of harmony led to the categorical distinction between "harmony" and "counterpoint." The other demanded the codification of the study of counterpoint, the establishment of a teaching method for which theorists had long groped and by which the didactic process was unequivocally subjected to historical perspective. It came to fruition in the *Gradus ad Parnassum* of Johann Joseph Fux.

Published in 1725 at imperial expense and distributed within a short time throughout the entire musical world, Fux's work marked a turning point in the evolution of music theory. "The earlier theorists either concentrate on the practice of their own time or, perhaps in accordance with long-established custom, follow the theories of their predecessors without considering contemporary practice. Fux, however, was fully aware that one is confronted with a choice in the matter of music theory; one does not learn everything from any one style-species. Every style has its particular technique, and therefore one must know exactly why he chooses some particular style rather than another as the basis of instruction. Most of the theorists of the sixteenth and seventeenth centuries, without giving the matter further consideration, based their work on the music about them and only occasionally made some comment to the effect that this or that idiom is beautiful or modern or that another is old-fashioned and less usable. Fux, however, leaves the music of his own time, the Bach-Handel epoch, and chooses consciously and with clear foresight the music of Palestrina as the basis of his teaching." [1]

The method of Fux's work is linked to the great past through essential style characteristics: the composing process on a given

[1] Knud Jeppesen, *Counterpoint*, p. 38. Using the classical form of the dialogue, Fux declares himself an apprentice of Palestrina in the text of his work; see the Author's Foreword to the Reader, below.

melody (cantus firmus); the emphasis on the melodic element resulting from consistently varied scale patterns (modes); the balance of consonance and dissonance determined by accent, preparation, and resolution; and the consideration of the vocal medium as the natural vehicle of musical composition as well as of performance. Fux discusses the study of counterpoint in two, three, and four parts, placing between the species of simple and florid counterpoint three intermediate species for the student's "graded" road to the Mountain of Muses.

Yet this extraordinary pedagogue was concerned with neither scholarly analysis nor speculative theory. We can understand his influence as an author only on the basis of the authority he commanded as a practicing musician. Fux was sixty-five years old when the *Gradus* appeared. In the position of director of court music in Vienna, the most distinguished musical office in his time, he had served as composer and conductor during the reign of three Habsburg emperors; he had also held the post of director of music at the cathedral of St. Stephen's. Universally respected and admired, he had himself become the "emperor of music." [2] By safeguarding the polyphonic tradition in an age in which its appreciation was fast waning, the Viennese master laid the foundation for a classical Viennese style. His foremost disciples were Haydn, Mozart, and Beethoven.

Haydn was a choirboy at St. Stephen's when Fux died, and it was ten years later that the young musician, "lacking means and a teacher"—the words from Fux's preface describe Haydn's situation—received his first systematic instruction in composition from the pages of Fux's *Gradus ad Parnassum*. "Haydn took infinite pains to assimilate the theory of Fux; he went through the whole work laboriously, writing out the exercises, then laying them aside for a few weeks, to look them over again later and polish them until he was satisfied he had done everything exactly right." [3] Haydn's

[2] P. H. Lang in *The Musical Quarterly*, April 1963, p. 254.
[3] G. A. Griesinger, *Biographische Notizen über Joseph Haydn*, p. 10.

copy of the *Gradus,* containing numerous manuscript annotations and preserved in the Esterházy Archives after Haydn's death, was destroyed in the Second World War. But a copy of Haydn's marginal entries made by the Haydn biographer C. F. Pohl has survived. In addition, a more explicit, though fragmentary Fux commentary by Haydn has come down to us in his *Elementarbuch,*[4] a condensation of Fux's study of counterpoint prepared for the purposes of Haydn's teaching. As Haydn's works show, his interest in contrapuntal techniques received a fresh impetus in the 1780s, the years of his close friendship with Mozart, and the plan of the *Elementarbuch* may have been prompted by various extracts of Fux's work in Mozart's hand, which date from the same period.

It is likely that Mozart studied Fux's work first under the influence of his father; the copy of the *Gradus* inscribed <<1746 Ex Libris Leopoldi Mozart>>, with annotations by Leopold Mozart, still exists in Salzburg. On the other hand, it has recently been ascertained that the studies based on Fux's cantus firmi, kept with this copy and for a long time thought to be Wolfgang's exercises written under Leopold's guidance, were actually written by one of Wolfgang's students under the latter's direction.[5] Mozart's own study of the *Gradus* may have been inspired or intensified through the instruction he received from Padre Martini (1770). We know that Martini's counterpoint lessons provided a decisive impulse for Mozart's work and that the Padre declared "We have no system other than that of Fux." [6] In any event, the only documents we

[4] *Elementarbuch der verschiedenen Gattungen des Contrapunkts. Aus den grösseren Werken des Kapellmeister Fux von Joseph Haydn zusammengezogen.* The work existed in different versions, two of which were used for the summary in Gustav Nottebohm, *Beethovens Studien* (1873). The only copy still extant is dated 1789 and was written by Haydn's pupil F. C. Magnus; it is preserved in the National Széchényi Library in Budapest.

[5] See Wolfgang Plath, "Beiträge zur Mozart-Autographie I," p. 112.

[6] Abbé Vogler, *Choral-System,* p. 6. Martini, like Gluck, had been in direct communication with Fux. An autograph draft for a letter that Martini wrote to Fux in praise of his work is attached to the *Gradus* copy from Martini's library (now in the *Liceo Musicale,* Bologna).

have of Mozart's work on Fux's text show Mozart not as a student but as a teacher—a fact that renders them of infinitely greater value to posterity. The most extensive among these manuscripts is the volume of studies that the English composer Thomas Attwood wrote as Mozart's student from 1785 to 1787 and that contains Mozart's corrections and comments as well as his copies and adaptations of models from Fux's text.[7]

A few weeks after Attwood had completed his studies with Mozart and returned to England, another young composer presented himself to Mozart with the hope of becoming his student—Beethoven. The hope was not to be fulfilled; Beethoven was called home, not to return to Vienna until five years later—a year after Mozart had died. His wish now, in the words of a farewell message from Count Waldstein, was to "receive Mozart's spirit from the hands of Haydn." Unavoidably, the implication of second choice was involved in the turn of events, and the association of Haydn and Beethoven, unlike that of Haydn and Mozart, was in fact awkward. Although a high personal and professional regard must have existed between the older and younger master, their relationship as teacher and student was not successful for the reason the modern observer might least suspect: Beethoven demanded a more systematic instruction than Haydn was, by age and temperament, disposed to give. Beethoven therefore decided to turn first to Johann Schenk, a minor Viennese composer, and later to Johann Georg Albrechtsberger, the distinguished friend and colleague of Haydn's, for tutelage. Each of the three teachers, nevertheless, based the course of studies upon the *Gradus ad Parnassum*, and Beethoven himself subsequently wrote out an *Introduction to Fux's Study of Counterpoint*.[8]

---

[7] *Thomas Attwoods Theorie- und Kompositionsstudien bei Mozart* (*Neue Mozart-Ausgabe, Serie X, Supplement, Werkgruppe* 30).

[8] Published, in shortened form, in Nottebohm's *Beethoveniana* (1872). Beethoven seems to have compiled the manuscript in 1809 for the instruction of Archduke Rudolph, the only student for whom he prepared an extensive set of lessons in composition.

With Beethoven's studies under Albrechtsberger, we enter upon a new phase of contrapuntal instruction. Directly connected with the tradition of Fux's work—he occupied Fux's post at St. Stephen's —Albrechtsberger departed at the same time from a basic premise of Fux's teaching. In his own writings, followed by many similarly oriented theoretical works, Albrechtsberger adapted the cantus firmus exercises of the *Gradus* to major and minor tonalities, and it was primarily in this modified form that the heritage of Fux reached the ever growing number of counterpoint students throughout the nineteenth century. Beethoven's studies were published in an edition compiled (with considerable license) by Ignaz Ritter von Seyfried, a fellow student under Albrechtsberger, and translated into French (by Fétis, 1833) and English (by Pierson, 1853). The list of subscribers to the French edition alone contains a remarkable collection of names: Cherubini, Berlioz, Meyerbeer, Chopin, Rossini, Auber, Paganini, Moscheles, Hummel, Liszt.

Through students of Albrechtsberger's school we can also follow the chain of his counterpoint instruction to Schubert, Bruckner, and Brahms. This last of the nineteenth-century Viennese masters, however, returned to the original form of Fux's work: Brahm's copy of the *Gradus* is preserved in Vienna together with the surviving copy of Haydn's *Gradus* annotations. The scholarly study of Fux's influence had begun in the second half of the nineteenth century with the work of the Viennese contrapuntists Nottebohm and Mandyczewski, and in the twentieth century Fux's text was revived in modern translations. Its use has continued in the hands of teachers of recent generations, among them Richard Strauss and Paul Hindemith; it has proved to be of a "practical significance which no other work on contrapuntal theory has attained." [9]

In choosing the Latin language, Fux insured a wide distribution for his work, but at the same time he placed before student and

[9] Jeppesen, *ibid.*

teacher the task of translating the *Gradus* into modern languages. The first to announce a translation was Telemann, the prolific master of Baroque music whose interest encompassed all musical trends of his time. Mattheson, Telemann's colleague and Fux's opponent in an earlier extended discussion of the modal system, hailed it in an "Ode upon seeing the announcement of a translation of Fux's Graduum ad Parnassum." [10] Yet Telemann's plan was apparently not carried out; the first published translation, a richly annotated German edition (1742), was prepared by Bach's student Lorenz Mizler "under the very eyes of Bach, as it were." [11] It was followed by a splendid Italian edition printed, like the original, in folio (Manfredi, 1761), and by a much more modest French version (Denis, 1773), which deviates considerably from Fux's text. The last of the eighteenth-century editions, published anonymously in English (1791), is a free paraphrase rather than a translation. The nineteenth century produced no translations of Fux's text; the next translations to follow were the German editions by the present writer (1938, 1951) and the version contained in this volume, published as the first English translation of Fux's text in 1943 (British edition 1944).

The complete text of the *Gradus* begins with an explanation of the nature of intervals and scales and ends with comments on various stylistic trends of Fux's time. The main body of the work consists of the study of counterpoint and fugue. The study of counterpoint forms an entity which is presented in this translation annotated with references to a number of works spanning the theoretical literature from Fux's time to our own. A complementary account of Fux's work, together with a translation of the discussion of fugal technique that follows the study of counterpoint in the *Gradus*, will be found in the *Study of Fugue* published by the present writer (1958; British edition 1959). A facsimile edition of

[10] *Grosse General-Bass-Schule* (1731), p. 172.
[11] Philipp Spitta, *J. S. Bach*, p. 125.

the complete Latin text, with English and German commentary, is planned for publication by the Johann-Joseph-Fux-Gesellschaft in the near future.

In prefacing a new edition of my English translation, I should like to make grateful acknowledgment of much kind help received. My thanks go to Paul Henry Lang, whose advice has guided the plan of an English translation from the outset, to Robert E. Farlow, vice president of W. W. Norton and Company, and to Nathan Broder, their music editor. For friendly assistance in making available new source material and information I am indebted to Dr. Jenö Vécsey and his staff at the National Széchényi Library in Budapest; to Dr. Hedwig Mitringer, Vienna; to Dr. Johann Harich, Eisenstadt; to Prof. Napoleone Fanti and Prof. L. F. Tagliavini, both of Bologna; to Prof. Hellmut Federhofer, Mainz; to Dr. Wolfgang Plath, Augsburg; and to Prof. Karl Geiringer, Santa Barbara, California. My gratitude is expressed again to Randall Thompson, to Willard Trask, to Mary Lago, and finally to John Edmunds, whose collaboration on the first edition of the English translation competently and delightfully aided the translator's first steps to the Parnassus of English prose. I regret that it was not possible to offer a revised text and enlarged commentary in the following pages. But in the hope that the present form of Fux's study of counterpoint will serve its new audience well, I shall borrow the celebrated author's postscript to the original preface: "If, benevolent reader, you should find departures from the proper manner of presentation, I trust you will accept them with even mind."

Westfield, New Jersey
    January, 1965   Alfred Mann

The Study of
Counterpoint

The Author's Foreword to the Reader

SOME PEOPLE will perhaps wonder why I have undertaken to write about music, there being so many works by outstanding men who have treated the subject most thoroughly and learnedly; and more especially, why I should be doing so just at this time when music has become almost arbitrary and composers refuse to be bound by any rules and principles, detesting the very name of school and law like death itself. To such I want to make my purpose clear. There have certainly been many authors famous for their teaching and competence, who have left an abundance of works on the theory of music; but on the practice of writing music they have said very little, and this little is not easily understood. Generally, they have been content to give a few examples, and never have they felt the need of inventing a simple method by which the novice can progress gradually, ascending step by step to attain mastery in this art. I shall not be deterred by the most ardent haters of school, nor by the corruptness of the times.

Medicine is given to the sick, and not to those who are in good health. However, my efforts do not tend—nor do I credit myself with the strength—to stem the course of a torrent rushing precipitously beyond its bounds. I do not believe that I can call back composers from the unrestrained insanity of their writing to normal standards. Let each follow his own counsel. My object is to help young persons who want to learn. I knew and still know many who have fine talents and are most anxious to study; however, lacking means and a teacher, they cannot realize their ambition, but remain, as it were, forever desperately athirst.

Seeking a solution to this problem, I began, therefore, many years ago, to work out a method similar to that by which children learn first letters, then syllables, then combinations of syllables, and fin-

ally how to read and write. And it has not been in vain. When I used
this method in teaching I observed that the pupils made amazing
progress within a short time. So I thought I might render a service
to the art if I published it for the benefit of young students, and
shared with the musical world the experience of nearly thirty years,
during which I served three emperors (in which I may in all modesty
take pride). Besides, as Cicero quotes from Plato: "We do not live
for ourselves alone: our lives belong also to our country, to our par-
ents, and to our friends."

You will notice, dear reader, that I have given very little space in
this book to theory and much more to practice, since (action being
the test of excellence) this was the greater need.

Finally, for the sake of better understanding and greater clarity,
I have used the form of dialogue. By *Aloysius*, the master, I refer
to Palestrina, the celebrated light of music, from Praeneste (or, as
others say, Praeeste), to whom I owe everything that I know of this
art, and whose memory I shall never cease to cherish with a feeling
of deepest reverence. By *Josephus* I mean the pupil who wishes to
learn the art of composition.

As for the rest, do not take offense at the humbleness of my style;
for I lay no claim to Latinity other than that of a voyager returning
to a land he once called home. And I would rather be understandable
than seem eloquent. Farewell, profit, and be indulgent.

The Dialogue

Josephus.— I come to you, venerable master, in order to be introduced to the rules and principles of music.

Aloysius.— You want, then, to learn the art of composition?

Joseph.— Yes.

Aloys.— But are you not aware that this study is like an immense ocean, not to be exhausted even in the lifetime of a Nestor? You are indeed taking on yourself a heavy task, a burden greater than Aetna. If it is in any case most difficult to choose a life work—since upon the choice, whether it be right or wrong, will depend the good or bad fortune of the rest of one's life—how much care and foresight must he who would enter upon this art employ before he dares to decide. For musicians and poets are born such. You must try to remember whether even in childhood you felt a strong natural inclination to this art and whether you were deeply moved by the beauty of concords.

Joseph.— Yes, most deeply. Even before I could reason, I was overcome by the force of this strange enthusiasm and I turned all my thoughts and feelings to music. And now the burning desire to understand it possesses me, drives me almost against my will, and day and night lovely melodies seem to sound around me. Therefore I think I no longer have reason to doubt my inclination. Nor do the difficulties of the work discourage me, and I hope that with the help of good health I shall be able to master it. I once heard a wise man say: Study is pleasure rather than a task.

Aloys.— I am happy to recognize your natural aptitude. There is only one matter that still troubles me. If this is removed I shall take you into the circle of my pupils.

Joseph.— Please say what it is, revered master. Yet surely neither this nor any other reason will move me to give up my plan.

Aloys.— Perhaps the hope of future riches and possessions in-
duces you to choose this life? If this is the case, believe me you must
change your mind; not Plutus but Apollo rules Parnassus. Whoever
wants riches must take another path.

Joseph.— No, certainly not. Please be sure that I have no other
object than to pursue my love of music, without any thought of gain.
I remember also that my teacher often told me one should be content
with a simple way of life and strive rather for proficiency and a good
name than for wealth, for virtue is its own reward.

Aloys.— I am delighted to have found just such a young student as I should wish. But tell me, are you familiar with everything
that has been said about the intervals, the difference between consonances and dissonances, about the different motions, and about
the four rules in the preceding book?

Joseph.— I believe I know all of this.

> (*I insert here the conclusion of the First Book, to
> which Fux refers:*)

[CONSONANCES

Unison, third, fifth, sixth, octave, and the intervals made up
of these and the octave are consonances. Some of these are perfect
consonances, the others imperfect. The unison, fifth, and octave are
perfect. The sixth and third are imperfect. The remaining intervals,
like the second, fourth,[1] diminished fifth, tritone, seventh, and the
intervals made up of these and the octave, are dissonances.

---

[1] In an earlier chapter, Fux distinguishes between the fourth obtained from the
arithmetical division of the octave [musical example] and that deriving from the harmonic
division [musical example] . (For harmonic and arithmetical division, see appendix, p. 141.)
In the first case, where the lower tone of the fourth is at the same time the fundamental tone—that is, in every instance when dealing with two voices—the fourth is
considered a dissonance. In the second case its dissonant character is invalidated by
the new fundamental tone, and it can be considered an imperfect consonance (see
p. 131). In classifying the fourth among the dissonances, Fux makes his decision with
regard to what he calls "a famous and difficult question." Martini, basing his opinion
upon that of Zarlino (*Institutioni Harmoniche*, Part III, ch. 5), goes so far as to call

These are the elements which account for all harmony in music. The purpose of harmony is to give pleasure. Pleasure is awakened by variety of sounds. This variety is the result of progression from one interval to another, and progression, finally, is achieved by motion. Thus it remains to examine the nature of motion.[2]

Motion in music denotes the distance covered in passing from one interval to another in either direction, up or down. This can occur in three ways, each of which is here illustrated:

DIRECT MOTION, CONTRARY MOTION, AND OBLIQUE MOTION

Direct motion results when two or more parts ascend or descend in the same direction by step or skip, as is shown in the example:

Direct Motion

FIG. 1

Contrary motion results when one part ascends by step or skip and the other descends—or vice versa; e.g.:

Contrary Motion

FIG. 2

the fourth a perfect consonance (*Esemplare*, pp. xv and 172). Haydn and Beethoven follow Fux. Mozart (*Fundamente des General-Basses*, p. 4) also lists the fourth as a dissonance.

[2] The statements, which introduce the following fundamental rules, may at the same time be considered an explanation of the principles of voice leading which they embody. The "variety of sound" is the basis from which all further rules are derived: first, the prohibition of parallel successions of perfect consonances, as depriving the voices of their independence; second, the rule that even imperfect consonances should be carefully used in parallel successions (not more than three or four following each other).

22

Oblique motion results when one part moves by step or skip while the other remains stationary, as seen in the examples:

Oblique Motion

Fig. 3

These three motions having been made clear, it remains to be seen how they are to be used in practice. This is set forth in the following four *fundamental rules*:

First rule: From one perfect consonance to another perfect consonance one must proceed in contrary or oblique motion.

Second rule: From a perfect consonance to an imperfect consonance one may proceed in any of the three motions.

Third rule: From an imperfect consonance to a perfect consonance one must proceed in contrary or oblique motion.

Fourth rule: From one imperfect consonance to another imperfect consonance one may proceed in any of the three motions.

Oblique motion, if used with due care, is allowed with all four progressions.[3]]

Aloys.— Let us settle down to work, then, and make a beginning in the name of Almighty God, the fountain of all wisdom.

Joseph.— Before we start on the exercises, revered master, may I still ask what one is to understand by the term *counterpoint?* I have heard this word used not only by musicians but also by laymen.

Aloys.— Your question is a good one, for this is to be the first subject of our study and work. It is necessary for you to know that in

---

[3] Beethoven (Nottebohm, *Beethoveniana*, I, p. 178) remarks that the four rules are, "strictly speaking, only two in number"; Martini (*Esemplare*, p. xxiii) reduces them to one: the only progression forbidden is the direct motion into a perfect consonance.

earlier times, instead of our modern notes, dots or points were used. Thus one used to call a composition in which point was set against or counter to point, *counterpoint*; this usage is still followed today, even though the form of the notes has been changed.[4] By the term counterpoint therefore is understood a composition which is written strictly according to technical rules. The study of counterpoint comprises several species which we shall consider in turn. First of all, then, the simplest species.

[4] Compare the explanation in Bellermann, *Contrapunkt*, p. 129.

FIRST PART

Chapter One

Note against Note

Joseph.— You have graciously answered my first question. Now will you tell me also—if you do not mind—what is meant by this first species of counterpoint, note against note?

Aloys.— I shall explain it to you. It is the simplest composition of two or more voices which, having notes of equal length, consists only of consonances. The duration of the notes is unimportant except that it should be the same for them all. Since the whole note, however, gives the clearest picture, I think we shall employ it in our exercises. With God's help, then, let us begin composition for two voices. We take as a basis for this a given melody [1] or cantus firmus, which we invent ourselves or select from a book of chorales, e.g.:

FIG. 4

To each of these notes, now, should be set a suitable consonance in a voice above; and one should keep in mind the motions and rules which are explained in the conclusion of the foregoing Book. Contrary and oblique motion should be employed as often as possible, since by their use we can more easily avoid mistakes. Greater care is needed in moving from one note to another in direct motion. Here,

[1] Principles for the forming of melodies are discussed later in the course of the work. The basic rule, however, from which all others are derived, might be mentioned beforehand: the possibility of vocal performance should always be taken into consideration. Therefore, no augmented, diminished, or chromatic intervals are to be used, nor intervals larger than the fifth (except for the octave and the minor sixth, which latter, however, should be employed only in an upward direction). Registers too high or too low (see p. 79), skips following each other in the same direction, and skips which are not compensated for subsequently should also be avoided.

because there is more danger of making a mistake, even closer attention should be paid to the rules.

Joseph.— As I know the motions and four rules, I think I understand everything you have just said. But I remember that you made a distinction between perfect and imperfect consonances. It may be necessary to know whether they must also be used differently.

Aloys.— Have patience, I shall explain everything. Certainly, there is a great difference between perfect and imperfect consonances, but I shall speak about this later. For the time being they may be employed impartially save for their different use according to the motions, and for the rule that more imperfect than perfect consonances should be employed. Excepted are the beginning and the end which both must consist of perfect consonances.

Joseph.— Would you mind explaining to me, dear master, why more imperfect than perfect consonances should be used here; and why the beginning and the end should be perfect consonances?

Aloys.— Your eagerness, which still is praiseworthy, forces me to explain almost everything in the wrong order. However, I shall answer your question though not yet discussing everything, so that you will not be confused by too many details at the beginning. The imperfect consonances, then, are more harmonious than perfect ones; the reason will be given at another time. Therefore, if a composition of this species, having only two parts and being otherwise very simple, too, should contain very many perfect consonances, it would necessarily be lacking in harmony. The rule concerning the beginning and the end is to be explained in this way: the beginning should express perfection and the end relaxation. Since imperfect consonances specifically lack perfection, and cannot express relaxation, the beginning and end must be made up of perfect consonances. Finally, it should be noticed that in the next to the last bar there must be a major sixth if the cantus firmus is in the lower part; and a minor third, if it is in the upper part.[2]

[2] Thus, the seventh degree has to be raised in the Dorian (D), Mixolydian (G), and Aeolian (A) modes. (The second degree of a mode occurs always as the next to

Joseph.— Is this all that is needed for this first species of counterpoint?

Aloys.— It is not all, but it is enough to begin with; the rest will become clear by the correction. To start then, take the cantus firmus as a basis and try to build upon it a counterpoint, using the soprano clef, and keeping in mind everything that has been said so far.

Joseph.— I shall do my best.

Fig. 5 [3]

Aloys.— You have done excellently; I am amazed at your intelligence and attention. But why did you put the numbers above the soprano and alto?

Joseph.— By the numbers above the alto I wanted to show the consonances I used in order to run less risk—by having the movement from one consonance to another before me—of missing the right kind of progression. The numbers above the soprano, 1, 2, 3, 4, 5, 6, 7, 8, etc., are only a numbering of the bars, so I can show you by them, revered master, that if I did correctly, it was not by accident but by design.

You told me the beginning should be a perfect consonance. I took one, choosing the fifth. From the first bar to the second, that is from a fifth to a third or from a perfect consonance to an imperfect one, I went by oblique motion, which progression, however, would

the last tone in the cantus firmus, the seventh degree always as the next to the last tone in the counterpoint.)

[3] For Fig. 5, *second and seventh bars:* The repetition of a tone—the only way of using oblique motion in the first species—may occur occasionally in the counterpoint; however, the same tone should not be repeated more than once.

have been possible by any of the three motions. From the second bar to the third, that is, from a third to a third, or from an imperfect consonance to an imperfect consonance, I chose parallel motion, according to the rule: from one imperfect consonance to another imperfect consonance one may go by any of the three motions. From the third bar to the fourth, or from a third, an imperfect consonance, to a fifth, a perfect one, I moved by contrary motion following the rule: from an imperfect consonance to a perfect consonance one must go in contrary motion. From the fourth bar to the fifth, or from a perfect consonance to an imperfect one, I used similar motion as the rule allows. From the fifth bar to the sixth, an imperfect consonance to a perfect one, contrary motion, since the rule calls for it. From the sixth bar to the seventh, oblique motion, where no mistake is possible. From the seventh bar to the eighth, an imperfect consonance to an imperfect consonance, parallel motion, as the rule permits. From the eighth bar to the ninth, an imperfect consonance to an imperfect consonance, I was free to choose any motion. From the ninth bar to the tenth the same thing held. The cantus firmus being in the lower voice the tenth pair of notes appearing next to the last is, as you advised, a major sixth. From the tenth bar to the eleventh, finally, I proceeded according to the rule which says: from an imperfect consonance to a perfect consonance one must move in contrary motion. The eleventh pair of notes, the conclusion, is, as you directed, a perfect consonance.

Aloys.— You show that you have done this with much thought. Therefore you may be certain, if only you master the three motions and four different rules thoroughly—so that with slight recourse to the memory you no longer make errors—the way for further progress is already open to you. Now go ahead; leave the cantus firmus in the alto clef and set a counterpoint below it in the tenor clef, though with this difference: that just as in the preceding example you have reckoned the consonances from the cantus firmus up, you now reckon them down from the cantus firmus to the lower part.

Joseph.— This seems more difficult to me.

Aloys.— It only appears so. I remember that other pupils, too, considered it harder. Yet it is not so bad provided you take care, as I told you, to reckon the consonances from the cantus firmus down to the lower part.

Fig. 6

Joseph.— Why did you mark a mistake in the first and second bar, venerable master? Have I not begun with a fifth, a perfect consonance? From that I went to the second pair of notes, a third, in direct motion, as the rule allows: from a perfect consonance to an imperfect consonance one may proceed in any of the three motions. Please help me out of my embarrassment; I am very ashamed.

Aloys.— Don't worry, my son, the first mistake did not happen through any fault of yours, since you did not know the rule that the counterpoint must be in the same mode as the cantus firmus; I was just about to explain it to you. Since, in this example, the cantus firmus is in D (*la, sol, re*) [4] as the beginning and conclusion show, and you started with G (*sol, re, ut*), you have obviously forced the beginning out of the mode. Because of this I have corrected the fifth to an octave, which establishes the mode as the cantus firmus.

Joseph.— I am glad that lack of knowledge and not inattention

[4] This quadruple denomination of the same tone derives from the old distribution of the tones into three hexachords (six-tone scales):

The hard hexachord (*hexachordum durum*)

The soft hexachord (*hexachordum molle*)

The natural hexachord (*hexachordum naturale*)

The degrees of each hexachord were called in turn, *ut, re, mi, fa, sol, la*, and it was customary to indicate the position of a tone in all three hexachords.

accounts for this mistake, which I certainly shall remember. But what kind of mistake have I made in the second bar?

Aloys.— The mistake does not occur in the progression from the first to the second bar but in that from the second to the third. You moved from the third to the fifth in direct motion against the rule: from an imperfect consonance to a perfect consonance one must go in contrary motion. This mistake is easily corrected. The lower voice remains, by means of oblique motion, on the low *d* (*la, sol, re*), so that a tenth results, in which case we are able to go from the second to the third pair of notes, i.e., from a tenth to a fifth, or from an imperfect consonance to a perfect one, in contrary motion, as the rule directs. This slight error need not worry you, because it is almost impossible for a beginner to be attentive enough to avoid every mistake. Practice is the key to all things. For the present be content that you have done the rest correctly—most of all, that you have put a minor third in the next to the last bar, since the cantus firmus is in the upper voice, as I had told you before.

Joseph.— Do you mind explaining to me the reason why one may not go from an imperfect consonance in direct motion to a perfect one, in order that I may understand this rule better and fix it more deeply in my memory?

Aloys.— Certainly. In this instance one may not do it because two fifths follow each other immediately, of which one is apparent or open, the other, however, concealed or hidden, and would stand out by the diminution of the interval, as I shall show you now in the example:

Fig. 7

This diminution a good singer would not make, especially in singing solo.[5] The same thing holds for the progression from the octave into the fifth in direct motion where two fifths would immediately follow each other, as is shown by the following example:

Fig. 8

You see, then, how by the diminution of the skip of the fifth, two fifths, one of which was concealed before, become apparent. From this you can recognize that the lawgivers of an art have set down nothing pointlessly and without deliberation.

Joseph.— I understand and am full of admiration.

Aloys.— Now continue the same exercise and go through all modes within this octave, just as they follow successively in their natural order. You started with *D*; thus *E, F, G, A* and *C* now follow.[6]

Joseph.— Why did you leave out *B* between *A* and *C*?

Aloys.— Because it has no perfect fifth and therefore cannot be the final of a mode—which we shall discuss more fully in its proper place.

Fig. 9

[5] This refers to the old practice of improvised ornamentation, especially the so-called diminution (filling out of intervals, and breaking up of large note values into smaller ones. Cf. pp. 41 and 51).

[6] I.e., the modes which begin on these tones.

This fifth is diminished and dissonant, since it consists of two whole tones and as many semitones, while the perfect, or consonant, fifth is made up of three whole tones and one semitone.

Joseph.— Couldn't one change the diminished fifth to a perfect one by flatting the lower note, or sharping the upper one, as in the following example?

FIG. 10

Aloys.— One may do so, but in this case, where the fifth leaves the diatonic system, it would no longer pertain to any of the natural modes—with which we shall now deal exclusively—but to a transposed mode, which will be discussed separately elsewhere.

Joseph.— Is there any distinction between these different modes?

Aloys.— Yes, a great difference. For the varying position of the semitones results in a different melodic line with each of these octaves. This, however, you need not know yet. So take your exercise up again, and try to find a counterpoint to the cantus firmus which I am writing down for you in *E*.

FIG. 11

You did very well. Now put the cantus firmus in the upper part and write a counterpoint below in the tenor clef.

Fɪɢ. 12

Joseph.— So I made a mistake again? If this befalls me in the two part composition of the simplest species, what will happen in the composition of three, four, and more parts? Please tell me what mistake is indicated by the bow from the sixth to the seventh bar and the cross above.

Aloys.— Don't worry about that mistake. You couldn't avoid it because your attention has not yet been called to it. And do not distress yourself in advance about writing for more voices, because practice will make you gradually more clear-sighted and skillful. Certainly you have often heard the well known verse:

mi against *fa*
is the devil in musica [7]

This *mi* against *fa* [8] you have written in the progression from the sixth to the seventh bar by a skip of an augmented fourth or tritone which is hard to sing and sounds bad, for which reason it is forbidden in strict counterpoint.[9] Now have confidence and go from *E* to the next mode, *F*:

[7] *Mi* (the third tone of a hexachord) and *fa* (the fourth tone of a hexachord) occur in most combinations of the different hexachords in the interval of a tritone or of a chromatic step, which makes their use in strict counterpoint impossible in these cases.

[8] *Fa*: the fourth tone of the natural hexachord, *f*; and *mi*: the third tone of the hard hexachord, *b*.

[9] The tritone is to be avoided even when reached stepwise if the line is not continued stepwise and in the same direction. The rule is less strict, however, when the tritone is brought about by the progressions of two voices:

See Jeppesen, *Counterpoint*, p. 100.

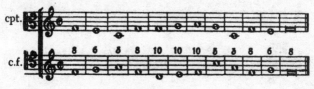

FIG. 13

Good, from beginning to end.

Joseph.— In this example you have set the cantus firmus in the tenor clef. Is there any special reason for that?

Aloys.— None, except that you should keep becoming more familiar with the different clefs. Here it is to be noticed that one should always use neighboring clefs in conjunction, so that the simple intervals can be distinguished more readily from the compound intervals.[10] Now, using the bass clef, write a counterpoint in the lower part to the cantus firmus.

FIG. 14

Right. But why did you allow the counterpoint to move above the cantus firmus from the fourth through the seventh bar?

Joseph.— Because otherwise I would have had to use direct motion up to this point, which would have resulted in less satisfactory voice leading.[11]

Aloys.— You did very well, especially as you have treated the cantus firmus in this instance, where it is simply like a lower voice, as

[10] A compound interval: the combination of a simple interval and the octave. The use of close position is essential for a balanced sound (cf. p. 112).

[11] Voice crossing will prove to be a very important expedient, especially in three and four part writing (see p. 100). Cf. Jeppesen, *Counterpoint*, p. 113.

a bass and have therefore reckoned the consonances from it. Now let us go on to G.

FIG. 15

Joseph.— I wrote the counterpoint with the closest attention and yet I see two marks for mistakes; from the ninth bar to the tenth and from the tenth to the eleventh.

Aloys.— You shouldn't be so impatient, though I am most glad about your care not to depart from the rules. But how should you avoid those small errors for which you have yet had no rules? From the ninth bar to the tenth you used a skip of a major sixth, which is prohibited in strict counterpoint where everything should be as singable as possible. Afterwards, from the tenth bar to the eleventh, you have brought together both voices from a tenth into an octave, leading them stepwise, the upper part down and the lower up. This octave, which is called *battuta* [12] by the Italians and *thesis* [13] by the Greeks—because it occurs at the beginning of the measure—is prohibited. I have long searched for the reason, but have found neither the nature of the mistake nor the difference that makes the octave in this example acceptable,

FIG. 16

12 Literally: "beaten."
13 Literally: "putting down." Both terms refer to the effect of a downbeat.

38

in the following one, however,

Fig. 17

not acceptable, since in both figures it is approached by contrary motion. It should be considered differently if the unison is reached in the same way, i.e., from the third, e.g.:

Fig. 18

In this case the voices, as they stand in the relation of absolute equality, would not be heard clearly enough and would seem to be null and void. On account of this the unison should nowhere be employed in this species of counterpoint, except at the beginning and the end. However, to return to the above-mentioned octave, the *battuta*, I shall leave to your discretion the use or avoidance of it; it is of little importance. But the approach from a more remote consonance into an octave by a skip is in my opinion not to be tolerated [14] even in the composition for more than two voices, e.g.:

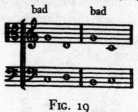

Fig. 19

The same holds true above all for the unison, e.g.:

[14] Cf. Roth, *Elemente der Stimmfuehrung*, p. 72, where *ottava* and *quinta battuta* mean only such progressions and are therefore definitely forbidden.

FIG. 20

In composition for eight voices similar skips can hardly be avoided in the basses or in the parts which take their place, as is to be discussed in its proper place. But we still need a counterpoint in the lower voice for the last example.

FIG. 21

Joseph.— What does the N.B. indicate at the first note of this example?

Aloys.— It means that the progression from the unison into another consonance by a skip is bad in itself, just as the progression into a unison is bad in itself, as I explained shortly before. Since this skip, however, appears in the part of the cantus firmus which is not to be changed, it may be tolerated here. It would be different if you were not confined to the cantus firmus, and the invention were left to your own choice. But why did you put a sharp in the eleventh bar? This is generally not used in the diatonic system.

Joseph.— I wanted to write a sixth here. But when I studied singing, I learned that *fa* leads down and *mi* leads up. Since the progression moves upward from the sixth into a third, I have used a sharp in order to emphasize the tendency to ascend. Besides, the *f* in the eleventh bar would result in a harsh relation with the *f♯* in the thirteenth bar.

40

Aloys.— You have been attentive. Now, I think every stumbling block is removed and you can proceed to the remaining modes, A and C:

FIGS. 22 AND 23

From the last two examples it is evident that you know everything necessary in this species of counterpoint. Let us now go on to the next.

Chapter Two

The Second Species of Counterpoint

BEFORE I take up the explanation of this species of counter-point you must know that here a binary meter is involved. The measure consists of two equal parts, the first of which is shown by the downbeat of the hand, the second, by the upbeat. The downbeat of the hand is called *thesis* in Greek, the upbeat, *arsis*, and I think that for greater convenience we should use these two terms in our exercises, too.[1] The second species results when two half notes are set against a whole note. The first of them comes on the downbeat and must always be consonant; the second comes on the upbeat, and may be dissonant if it moves from the preceding note and to the following note stepwise. However, if it moves by a skip, it must be consonant. In this species a dissonance may not occur, except by diminution, i.e., by filling out the space between two notes that are a third distant from each other, e.g.:

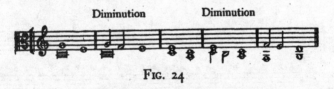

FIG. 24

It makes no difference whether the note which results from the diminution is consonant or dissonant; it is satisfactory if the space between the two notes, a third distant from each other, is filled out.

Joseph.— Aside from this, must one follow what has been

---

[1] I have used "downbeat" and "upbeat," since these words have acquired currency as musical terms in English. Generally, the two Greek terms are used in the reverse, thesis for upbeat, and arsis for downbeat (even in Bellermann and Jeppesen). This can be explained by the fact that Fux derives his terms from the raising and lowering of the arm whereas usually they are derived from the raising or lowering of the voice.

prescribed in the first species of counterpoint concerning motion and progression?

Aloys.— Yes, certainly; except that in this species the next to the last measure should have a fifth, followed by a major sixth, if the cantus firmus—or chorale melody—is in the lower voice. If the cantus firmus is in the upper voice, there should be a fifth followed by a minor third. The example will make this clear:

FIG. 25

It will be very helpful if you consider the ending before you start to write. Now let us proceed, taking the same cantus firmi.

Joseph.— I shall try. But I hope you will be patient if I make mistakes; I still have very little knowledge in this matter.

Aloys.— Do as well as you can; I shall not mind. The corrections will clarify whatever may be obscure to you.

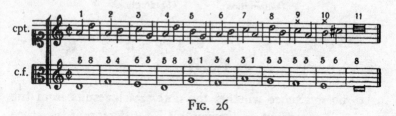

FIG. 26

Joseph.— My fear of making mistakes was not unfounded. I see two marks for mistakes; one at the first note of the ninth bar, and the other at the first note of the tenth bar, and I do not know what is wrong in either case. Both times I moved from an imperfect consonance to a perfect consonance by contrary motion.

Aloys.— You reason correctly. There are two mistakes of the same kind. However, you could not have known this since you had not yet been told about it. It should be said that the skip of a third cannot prevent a succession of either two fifths or two octaves. The intervening note on the upbeat is regarded as hardly existing, since owing to its short duration and the small distance between the tones it cannot compensate to such an extent that the ear will not notice the two succeeding fifths or octaves. Let us consider the example again, beginning from the eighth bar.

FIG. 27

If we disregard the intervening note which occurs on the upbeat, those measures would appear thus:

FIG. 28

The same holds for octaves:

FIG. 29

It is different if the skip is of a greater interval; e.g., a fourth, fifth, or sixth. In such a case the distance between the two tones causes the

44

ear to forget, as it were, the first note on the downbeat until the next note on the downbeat. Let us look once at the last example with the intervening skip of a fourth invalidating the succession of octaves.

Fig. 30

It is on this account, too, that I did not mark as wrong the progression from the third measure to the fourth; for if one did not take into account the intervening note the passage would appear thus:

Fig. 31

This progression would be against the rule which says: from an imperfect consonance to a perfect consonance one must proceed in contrary motion. However, the mistake is avoided by the skip of a fourth in this manner:

Fig. 32

Now correct your previous exercise.

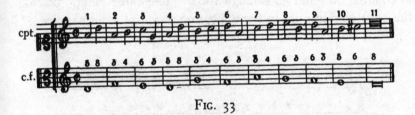

FIG. 33

I see that you have sufficiently understood everything that has been explained so far. Still, before you go on to set an example with the counterpoint in the lower voice, I should like to point out some devices which it will be very useful for you to know. First, one may use a half rest in place of the first note. Second, if the two parts have been led so close together that one does not know where to take them; and if there is no possibility of using contrary motion, this motion can be brought about by using the skip of a minor sixth (which is permissible) or an octave, as in the following examples:

FIG. 34

Go on, now, and work out the same exercise with the counterpoint in the lower voice.

FIG. 35

Now take all the cantus firmi which were given for the first species of counterpoint and go through the five remaining modes, placing the counterpoint once in the upper and once in the lower voice.

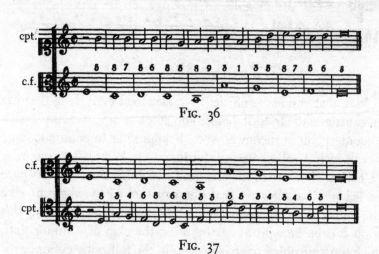

FIG. 36

FIG. 37

Joseph.— I remember you recently said that in the next to the last measure there should first be a fifth, if the counterpoint occurs in the lower voice in this species. But obviously, in this mode the fifth, being dissonant, may not be used on account of *mi* against *fa*. Therefore I wrote a sixth rather than a fifth.

Aloys.— I am very pleased to find you so careful. Go on now, writing the same exercise in the four remaining modes.

FIG. 38

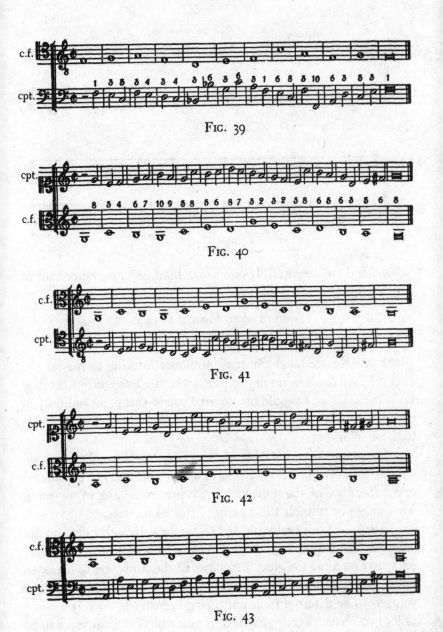

FIG. 39

FIG. 40

FIG. 41

FIG. 42

FIG. 43

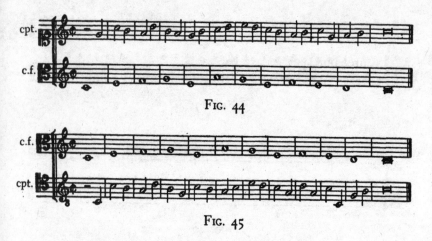

Fig. 44

Fig. 45

You have done very well. If one works hard one may be certain of God's help. Always remember:

> drops wear down the stone
> not by strength but by constant falling.

Therefore, we are taught to work tirelessly in order to master the sciences, and to allow no day to pass without a line written (as they say). In addition, I should like to urge you at this point not only to pay attention to the measure upon which you are working but also to those following.

Joseph.— Yes, venerable master, I could scarcely have known what to do in the last counterpoint exercises if I had not considered one or another of the measures in advance, weighing in my mind what might be suitable there before I started to write.

Aloys.— I am really pleased to see how thoughtfully you are working. Yet I want to remind you again and again to make every effort to overcome the great difficulties of the study you have undertaken; and neither to become discouraged by hard work, nor to allow yourself to be deterred from unflagging industry by flattery of such skill as you have already achieved. If you will work thus you will be delighted to see the way in which light gradually illuminates what had been obscure and how in some manner the curtain of darkness seems to be drawn away.

As for the rest, ternary time has yet to be mentioned here; in this case three notes are set against one. Since this is not a very difficult matter, and therefore of little significance, I think it is not necessary to trouble to arrange a special chapter dealing with it. We shall find that a few examples will suffice to make it clear.

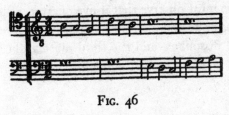

FIG. 46

Here the middle note may be dissonant because all three of them move stepwise. It would be different if one note or the other moved by skip, in which case all three notes would have to be consonant, as should be apparent from what I have already said.

Chapter Three

The Third Species of Counterpoint

BY THE third species of counterpoint is meant a composition having four quarters against a whole note. Here, in the first place, one must observe that if five quarters follow each other either ascending or descending, the first one has to be consonant, the second may be dissonant, and the third must again be consonant. The fourth one may be dissonant if the fifth is consonant, as is shown in the examples: [1]

FIG. 47

This does not hold if, firstly, the second and fourth notes are consonant, in which case the third note may be dissonant, as in the following examples:

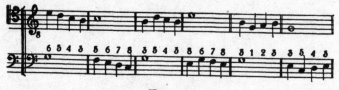

FIG. 48

Here the third note is always dissonant, and may be described as a diminution or a filling out of the skip of the third. In order to show

[1] Roth, *Elemente der Stimmfuehrung*, p. 77, cites as the only exception

, a passage already mentioned in Martini, *Esemplare*, p. xxvi.

this process more clearly we should change these examples back to their original forms:

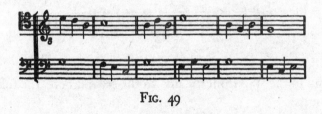

FIG. 49

From this one may see that the third note, the dissonance, in the previous examples is nothing but a diminution of the skip of a third. It fills in the space from the second note to the third, which space can always be filled in by a diminution, i.e., by supplying the intervening note.

The second instance in which one departs from the general rules is that of the changing note, which is called *cambiata* [2] by the Italians. It occurs if one goes from the second note—when dissonant —to a consonant note by skip, as is to be seen by the following examples:

FIG. 50

Strictly speaking, the skip of a third from the second note to the third note should occur from the first to the second note; in this case the second note would form a consonant sixth.

---

[2] Literally: the "exchanged note." This is the first mention ever made in musical literature of the *nota cambiata*, though it had been in use since the early days of polyphony.

52

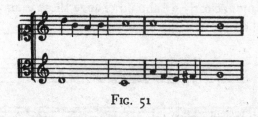

FIG. 51

If we fill in the skip from the first to the second note, the following line results:

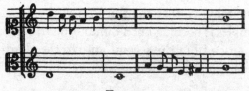

FIG. 52

Since in this species, however, eighth notes are not yet to be employed, the old masters have approved the first example where the second note forms a seventh [3]—possibly because it is easier to sing.[4]

Finally, I have to show how the next to the last measure should be treated, it being as usual more difficult than the others. If the cantus firmus occurs in the lower part, there are these possibilities:

FIG. 53

If the cantus firmus occurs in the upper part, the possibilities are these:

[3] Or fourth, respectively.—*Marginal note in the original.*

[4] The skip from an accented to an unaccented note was considered difficult to sing when dealing with smaller note values (especially in an upward direction; see Jeppesen, *Das Sprunggesetz des Palestrinastils bei betonten Viertelnoten*).

FIG. 54

If you know this and, in addition, keep in mind what has been said already of the other species you will have no difficulty with this species. Still, I want to remind you again to pay the utmost attention to measures following; otherwise, you may sometimes find yourself unable to go on. Now start to work, taking in turn all the cantus firmi used in the first lesson: [5]

FIG. 55

FIG. 56

FIG. 57

[5] Here, as in the preceding species, it is possible to use a rest instead of the first note in the counterpoint, thus stressing the independence of the two lines; cf. Fig. 132.

54

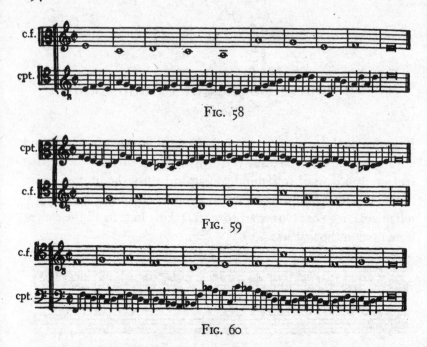

c.f.

cpt.

FIG. 58

cpt.

c.f.

FIG. 59

c.f.

cpt.

FIG. 60

Why did you use flats in some places? They usually do not occur in the diatonic system with which we are now dealing.

Joseph.— I thought that otherwise harsh relations might occur because of *mi* against *fa*, and it seemed to me that these flats would not interfere with the diatonic system since they were not used functionally, but nonessentially.

Aloys.— You have worked very carefully. For the same reason sharps sometimes have to be used; when and where they are to be used, however, must be considered carefully. From the last examples it appears that you know everything required for this species. I leave it to you to work out the three remaining modes, G, A, and C, by yourself so that we shall not be detained too long. Let us proceed, therefore, to

[6] For Fig. 58: The forming of sequences (the so-called monotonia) ought to be avoided as far as possible. In the original the following correction for the next to the last measure was added in manuscript:

Chapter Four

The Fourth Species of Counterpoint

IN THIS species there are two half notes set against a whole note. These half notes are on one and the same tone and are connected by a tie, the first of which must occur on the upbeat, the second on the downbeat. This species is called *ligature* or *syncopation*, and can be either consonant or dissonant. The consonant ligature results when both half notes, the one on the upbeat and that on the downbeat, are consonant. The examples will make this clear:

Consonant Ligatures

FIG. 61

The dissonant ligature results when the half note on the upbeat is consonant (which must always be the case); the half note on the downbeat, however, is dissonant, as is to be seen from the following examples:

Dissonant Ligatures

FIG. 62

Since the dissonances here do not occur nonessentially—by diminution—as in the preceding examples, but functionally, and on the downbeat; and since they cannot please by themselves, being offensive to the ear, they must get their euphony from the resolution into the following consonance. Therefore, something now has to be said about

THE RESOLUTION OF DISSONANCES

Before I proceed to explain the manner in which dissonances are to be resolved, you should know that the notes held over and, as it were, bound with fetters, are nothing but retardations of the notes following, and thereafter proceed as if brought from servitude into freedom. On this account dissonances should always resolve descending stepwise to the next consonances, as is to be seen from the following example.

FIG. 63

This figure, if the retardation were removed, would appear thus:

FIG. 64

From this, one can see that it is easy to find the consonance into which any dissonance must resolve; that is to say, it must be resolved to the consonance which would occur on the downbeat of the following measure if the retardation were removed. Therefore, if the cantus firmus is in the lower voice, the interval of the second must be resolved to the unison, that of the fourth to the third, that of the seventh to the sixth, and that of the ninth to the octave. Because of this it is not permissible to proceed either from the unison to the second or from the octave to the ninth when using ligatures, as is shown in the following examples:

Fig. 65

For if the retardations are removed an immediate succession of two unisons would result in the first instance, and an immediate succession of two octaves in the second instance.[1]

Fig. 66

It is quite the contrary if one goes from the third to the second or from the tenth to the ninth:

Fig. 67

[1] In the case of fifths, however, the retardation can mitigate the effect of parallel motion. Successions of fifths may therefore be used with syncopations (see p. 95).

These passages are correct because they sound well even if the retardations or ligatures are removed:

FIG. 68

Now that it has been shown which dissonances one may use and how they must be resolved if the cantus firmus occurs in the lower voice, it remains to be explained which dissonances may be used if the cantus firmus occurs in the upper voice, and how they are there to be resolved. I should like to say, therefore, that one may use here the second resolving to the third, the fourth resolving to the fifth, and the ninth resolving to the tenth, e.g.:

FIG. 69

Joseph.— Why do you omit the seventh? Is it not possible to use it if the cantus firmus is in the upper voice? Please do not resent my asking the reason.

Aloys.— I have intentionally omitted the seventh. However, there is hardly any reason to be given except the model of the great masters, to which we should always pay the utmost attention in our work. There is no one among them who has used the seventh resolving in this way to the octave:

Fig. 70

One might say, perhaps, that this resolution of the seventh is not good because it moves into a perfect consonance, the octave, from which it gets too little euphony. But in the same great masters one frequently finds the second, the inversion of the seventh, resolved to the unison, from which, as the most perfect of all consonances, a dissonance may gain much less euphony. It seems to me that here one should follow the practice of the great masters. Let us consider the example of the seventh inverted to the second and resolved to the unison.

Fig. 71

Joseph.— Before I begin the exercises may I ask, if you don't mind, whether the retardation or ligature into the dissonance is also to be used in ascending? It seems to me that a like matter is dealt with in the following examples:

Fig. 72

60

Aloys.— You raise a problem which is harder to untangle than the Gordian knot. I shall deal with it later because, being still at the threshold of the art, you would not now wholly understand it. Although it may seem to be a matter of indifference whether a series of thirds ascends or descends, if you remove the retardation, yet there remains a certain distinction. This, as I said, will be explained sometime separately.[2] For the time being, as your teacher I advise you to resolve all dissonances down to the next consonance. For the rest, in this species a seventh resolving into the sixth should appear in the next to the last measure if the cantus firmus is in the lower voice. If the cantus firmus is in the upper voice one should conclude with a second resolving to a third and finally moving into the unison.

Joseph.— Should there be a ligature in every measure?

Aloys.— In general, yes, wherever possible. However, one will occasionally come upon a measure where no ligature can be introduced. In such a case one must write plain half notes until there is an opportunity to use syncopation again. So start with the ligatures:

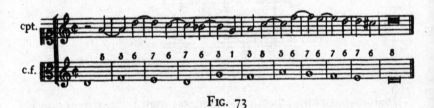

Fig. 73

Right. But why did you leave out the ligature in the fifth measure? You could have used one if you had written a fifth after the third. This would have been the first note of the ligature; then, staying on the same line, you would have had a sixth on the downbeat of the following measure as the second note of the ligature. I told you that one should not miss any occasion for using a syncopation.

Joseph.— Yes. But here I did so intentionally, in order to avoid

[2] The best and simplest explanation of this is the natural law of gravity; see Roth, *Elemente der Stimmfuehrung*, p. 89.

a bad repetition. I had used the same ligatures immediatcly before in the third and fourth measures.

Aloys.— That is very observant and thoughtful, because one should equally consider ease of singing and correctness of the progressions. Now go on:

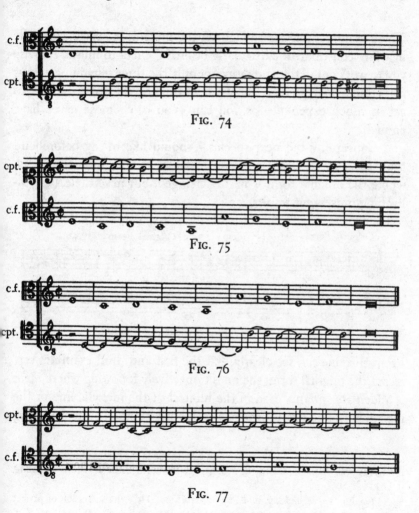

FIG. 74

FIG. 75

FIG. 76

FIG. 77

FIG. 78

These examples may be enough for the present. However, since the ligatures contribute a particularly beautiful effect to music, I advise you to work out in the same way not only the three remaining cantus firmi, but also to go over the others in this species again, in order to get as much experience as you can—you can almost never have enough.

Concerning the next species I should like to say beforehand that the ligatures discussed so far may also be used in another way, where the original form is hardly changed, but nevertheless an enlivening movement results, e.g.:

FIG. 79

From this one can see clearly that the first and third examples represent the original form; the ones respectively following where *idem* is added are variants used in the interest of the melodic line or the movement. The ligatures may also be interrupted in the following way:

[3] For Fig. 74: A dependence of the counterpoint upon the cantus firmus, as appears in this example, should ordinarily be avoided; see Roth, *Elemente der Stimmfuehrung*, p. 104.

[4] For Fig. 75, *second bar,* and Fig. 77, *tenth bar*: Here the succession of perfect consonances is to be considered more indulgently than in Fig. 65; cf. Figs. 146, 147, 200, 201.

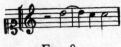

Fig. 80

Furthermore, two eighths may occasionally be used in the next species; that is, on the second and fourth beats of the measure—but never on the first and third.

Fig. 81

If you have understood this let us go on to

Chapter Five

The Fifth Species of Counterpoint

THIS species is called florid counterpoint. As a garden is full of flowers so this species of counterpoint should be full of excellences of all kinds, a plastic melodic line, liveliness of movement, and beauty and variety of form. Just as we use all the other common species of arithmetic—counting, addition, multiplication and subtraction—in division, so this species is nothing but a recapitulation and combination of all the preceding ones. There is nothing new that need be explained, except that one should take the utmost care to write a singable, melodic line—a concern I beg you always to keep in mind.

Joseph.— I shall do my best, but I hardly dare to take up the pen, not having any example before me.

Aloys.— Be of good heart; I shall give you the first example:

Fɪɢ. 82

Fɪɢ. 83

Following these models you may work out the counterpoints to the remaining cantus firmi.

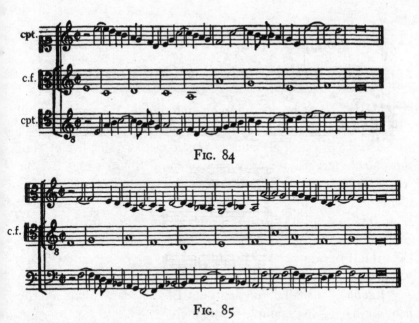

FIG. 84

FIG. 85

You have worked very diligently and what pleases me particularly is that you have not only paid close attention to writing a good melodic line but have also, in approaching the downbeats, made use of oblique motion—or syncopations—in most instances. This expedient I should like to recommend to you further, since it brings about the greatest beauty in counterpoint.

Joseph.— I am very happy to see that you are not altogether dissatisfied with my efforts, and I am sure that with such encouragement I shall soon reap a good harvest. Shall I work out the remaining modes in your presence, or by myself?

Aloys.— As this species is more valuable than I can possibly say, I wish you would take up these three modes in my presence. In general, I want to urge you to work constantly and with special diligence in this species above all others.[1]

Joseph.— I shall always follow your advice as law.

---

[1] See Jeppesen, *Counterpoint*, p. xv.

Fig. 86

Fig. 87

Fig. 88

What does the N.B. in the fifth measure of the upper voice indicate in the last example?

Aloys.— Do not let it disturb you, for you have not yet been told about it. But let me tell you now, not as a rule but by way of advice: since the melodic line seems to lag if two quarters occur at the beginning of the measure without a ligature following immediately, it will be better—if one wants to write two quarters at the beginning of the measure—to connect them by a ligature with the notes following, or else to make it easier for these two quarters to go on by using some additional quarters, as is shown in the example.

FIG. 89

Now, we have completed the exercises in two part counterpoint upon a cantus firmus, having gone through all five species—for which we should be duly thankful to God. We have now to return to the beginning; that is, to note against note in three part composition, and to see what must here be taken into consideration in each species, and how three part composition is to be managed.

SECOND PART

Chapter One

Note against Note in Three Parts

THAT three part composition is the most perfect of all is already evident from the fact that in it one can have a complete harmonic triad without adding another voice. If a fourth voice or more voices are added, this is, so to speak, only a repetition of another voice already present in the harmonic triad. Hence it has become almost a proverb that to those who master three part composition the way to the composition of more parts is made quite easy.

Joseph.— I am most anxious to know how this kind of composition is to be written, though I am rather afraid that there will be many difficulties to hinder me.

Aloys.— There is no need to worry; since you have not had too hard a time working through the species of two part composition you may be certain that it will not be unduly difficult for you to write in three parts. Just be sure you understand what I am about to tell you now, and begin with the simplest species, note against note, proceeding in the order we have observed in two part composition.

This species, then, is the simplest combination of three voices and consists of equal notes, or more precisely, of three whole notes in each instance, the upper two being consonant with the lowest.[1]

Here it is to be observed first of all that the harmonic triad should be employed in every measure if there is no special reason against it.

Joseph.— What is the harmonic triad?

Aloys.— It is a combination of the intervals of the third and the fifth,[2] e.g.:

[1] Cf. p. 112.

[2] Fux applies the term harmonic triad only to a chord is position: $\frac{5}{3}$, not to the inversions of this chord for which, today, the term triad so used. 1

FIG. 90

Joseph.— And why is it sometimes impossible to use this triad?

Aloys.— Occasionally, for a better melodic line, one uses a consonance not properly belonging to the triad, namely, a sixth or an octave. More often the necessity of avoiding the succession of two perfect consonances demands the giving up of the triad and the use of a sixth instead of the fifth, or of an octave; or of both of them [3] —as I shall show you in the following example:

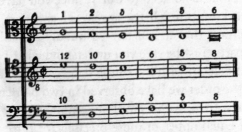

FIG. 91

[3] I.e., $\frac{6}{1}$ $\frac{8}{1}$ or $\frac{8}{1}$ or $\frac{6}{1}$ instead of $\frac{5}{1}$. This statement indicates the difference between this school, which springs from voice leading, and the later ones, which are influenced by harmonic principles. The chords $\frac{8}{1}$ and $\frac{8}{1}$ are here considered equal in use; no attention is paid to the change of root.

Joseph.— With your permission, dear master, may I say that in the second measure the triad seems to have been avoided without any apparent reason? I think one could have used the fifth, completing the triad in the tenor. Then, in the third measure, the tenor might have taken the third, and the other bars could have remained as you have written them:

FIG. 92

The course of the voice does not seem to interfere either with the correctness of the progression, nor does it make the melodic line less singable.

Aloys.— Your alteration is not bad and your example is not to be considered wrong. But who cannot see that the first—that is, my example—follows the natural order and the principle of variety more closely? It takes the natural order more strictly into account because the tenor moves down gracefully, stepwise without any skip, through the third measure where there is a sixth. This interval combines better than any other with the note *mi*,[4] if this occurs in the bass. This has already been explained, but it should be explained again in more detail. Let us first take this chord with the sixth:

[4] The third degree.

FIG. 93

This note which determines the sixth should be considered as if it were moved from its proper place to an unusual one. If it were in its proper place the chord would appear thus:

FIG. 94

This *c*, as it occurs in its proper place, establishes the harmonic triad. If it is transposed an octave higher and the other voices remain where they are, a sixth will necessarily result. This holds true especially if the *mi* is followed by *fa*, as in this example:

FIG. 95

However, if *mi* goes to another note it requires the fifth rather than the sixth,[5] as in the following example:

---

[5] For this will result in better voice leading, especially in the soprano.

FIG. 96

Now let us return from our digression to a consideration of the reasons why my example takes variety, too, more into account. The note *a* occurs there only once in the tenor whereas it occurs twice in your example, as you can readily see:

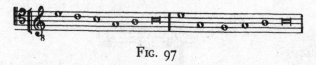

FIG. 97

I should like to tell you again, at this point, that one should always take great care to have this sort of variety.

Joseph.— Please do not resent it if I ask why you began the example you gave me a little while ago with the voices so far apart. I think it could also have been done otherwise.

Aloys.— I don't mind at all; on the contrary, I am delighted by your eagerness to learn. Haven't you noticed that in this example the bass ascends consistently stepwise? In order to allow enough space for the voices to move toward each other by contrary motion, the upper voices had at the beginning to be thus distant from the bass. But how would you suggest that the example be amended?

Joseph.— I should like to write two examples—not in order to amend but in order to learn.

FIG. 98

Aloys.— I do not find your examples altogether bad. But you see that in the first example, from the first bar to the second, all voices ascend, partly by step, partly by skip; a progression which can hardly be managed without awkwardness resulting. Here it results when the tenor together with the alto takes this course from the first bar to the second:

FIG. 99

From this it is clear that if the bass is taken out the progression is obviously bad, not only because it moves, so to speak, from an imperfect consonance to a perfect one, but—and this is worse—because this fifth is not even perfect, but diminished. The rules should be observed reckoning not from the bass alone but, if possible, also from any one part to any other, although this is not very strictly applied in composition of several parts. Already in three part composition one may depart from the rigorous observance of the rules in leading the other voices above the bass if there is a serious reason for doing so. You can see this in the next to the last bar of the previous example where there is a progression from the fifth to the final octave, that is, from a perfect consonance into another perfect consonance by direct motion, because there is no other possibility.

FIG. 100

Joseph.— Could this awkwardness not have been avoided by taking a tenth instead of the octave?

Aloys.— Yes, perhaps; however, one feels that the degree of perfection and repose which is required of the final chord does not become sufficiently positive with this imperfect consonance. It is otherwise in four part composition where these conditions may be fulfilled when the fifth is added, the third being no longer too prominent.

Joseph.— But what do you find wrong in my second example?

Aloys.— Nothing except that the ascending sixths on the downbeat sound rather harsh. If they occur on the upbeat (which, however, has no place in this species) they are more tolerable since they seem to be less distinct—as will be explained more fully at another time.

Now let us proceed to our exercises. To make it easier for you to work in this species by having a model before you, I will write the first example for you, which, corresponding to the three parts, shall be threefold: first the cantus firmus will occur in the upper voice, then in the middle, and finally in the lower voice. And I wish you to follow the same procedure when you take up the cantus firmi in the order in which they were given before.

FIG. 101

From this you may see that the harmonic triad has been employed in each measure if there is no special reason against it, and furthermore that care has been taken to insure such proper progressions and motions as have already been repeatedly mentioned.

Joseph.— Still, from the seventh measure to the eighth it looks, in the alto and bass parts, as if you have not observed the rule: from an imperfect consonance to a perfect consonance one must proceed in contrary motion. You have used direct motion instead.

Aloys.— That is so. But you must remember I said a little while ago that, if there is no other possibility, one may occasionally depart from the strict rules in three part composition, in order to avoid a worse awkwardness.

Joseph.— Yes, I know. But I think that, while still observing the rules strictly, one could yet make it satisfactory by going from the *f* in the bass to the high *c*, thus continuing a progression in contrary motion.

FIG. 102

Aloys.— That would take care of the bad passage. But don't you see that in this way two progressions of the same kind [6] follow immediately; from the ninth bar to the tenth, and from the tenth bar to the last? Moreover, in the ninth bar the tenor and bass parts, as you see, blend in a unison, which is less harmonious than the octave. Besides, in this sort of composition one should not exceed the limits of the five lines without grave necessity.[7]

Joseph.— I feel myself to be almost entirely refuted by these reasons. But perhaps it would have been possible to write it thus?

Fig. 103

Aloys.— No, that would be even less acceptable. Don't you remember that the skip of the major sixth is prohibited? What, then, would you say about the skip of the seventh? Remember that one has to take singableness into account. Now I shall give you an example in which the cantus firmus is in the middle voice:

Fig. 104

[6] Hidden fifths and octaves.

[7] The old clefs encompassed the respective natural ranges of the human voice. Here

Joseph.— Why have you written an octave in the ninth measure? I think one might without any difficulty have used a fifth and thus the harmonic triad.

Aloys.— Yes, that would have been possible. But, looking a little more carefully, you will find that the octave takes the singable line more into account—a consideration which should always be kept in mind, as I have already said and shall often have to say again. Now the example with the cantus firmus in the lower voice still remains to be written:

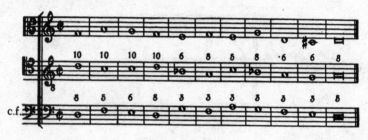

FIG. 105

Joseph.— There is nothing that is unclear to me in this example except the last measure. It seems to me that this chord would have been more harmonious if there were a third instead of a fifth.

Aloys.— You are right. But which third do you think one should take—the major or the minor? If you mean the minor third don't you realize that it is not capable of giving a sense of conclusion? [8] And if you mean the major third, don't you realize that the mode itself contains the minor third, that is, *f* without the sharp, and that the ear therefore has become accustomed to this characteristic of the melodic line throughout the course of the cantus firmus and would be somewhat disturbed by the raised third at the end? Therefore it is advisable to omit the third altogether.

Now start to work out the examples in the five remaining modes,

it is again inferred that the principles of vocal writing ought to be the basic principles of composition.

[8] Cf. Martini, *Esemplare*, p. 14.

setting the cantus firmus in all three voices in turn, as I have already said and shown, and always keeping in mind what has been explained thus far.

FIG. 106

Joseph.— I had some trouble in working out the final cadence. Since in the chord of the next to the last measure the regular cadence

FIG. 107

cannot be used, and since in this place the mode does not provide a perfect fifth nor admit of any raising by which an ordinary cadence might be achieved, it seems to me that it is not possible to close otherwise than as I did. Still, I am not sure about the major third I used in the last measure. I remember that you said just now that the third is to be omitted altogether in such modes and the fifth used in its place.

Aloys.— You used good judgment about this cadence. The unusual position of the semitone does require an unusual cadence and on this account the regular cadence cannot be employed. Concerning the use of the third in the final chord you should have no

82

misgivings, because what I told you regarding the omission of the third holds true only in cases in which it is possible. You have rightly recognized that one cannot use the fifth in the last bar of this example without an immediate succession of two fifths resulting, and that, because of this, one must take a major third instead; for the minor third being a more perfect consonance is still less suitable for the end.

Now go on.

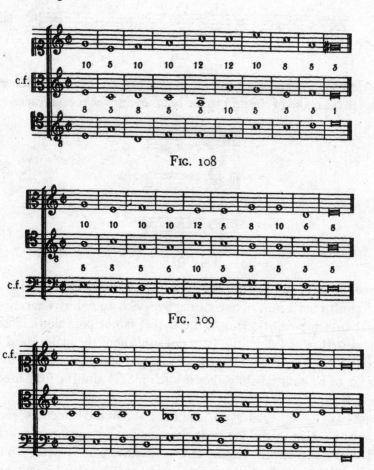

Fig. 108

Fig. 109

Fig. 110

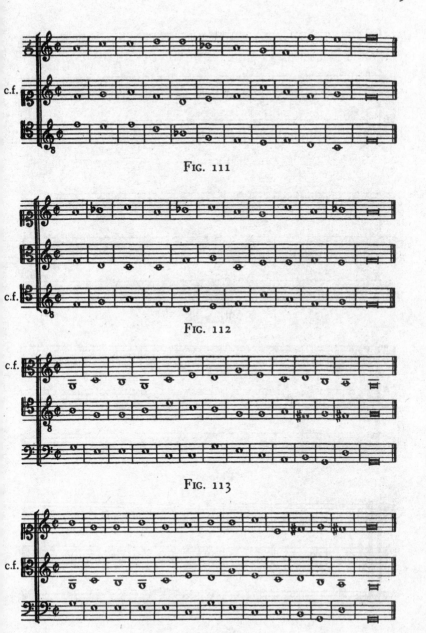

FIG. 111

FIG. 112

FIG. 113

FIG. 114

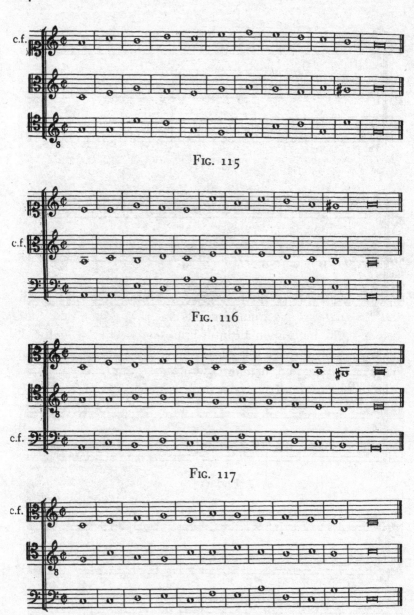

FIG. 115

FIG. 116

FIG. 117

FIG. 118

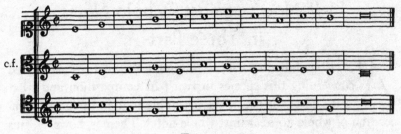

FIG. 119

Joseph.— These examples in the remaining modes are worked out as well, I think, as the limitation of the cantus firmus allows. Perhaps the composition might have been enriched by the harmonic triad in many places, if the need for following the cantus firmus had not restricted the liberty of composing.

Aloys.— That is right; and in good time when you are ready to write free composition you will no longer be troubled by being restricted to the cantus firmus. But it is almost incredible how useful such exercises, built upon a cantus firmus, are to him who pursues this study. Only through this knowledge and practice will he be able to master this art, and therefore I want to recommend to you—and it cannot be urged too often—that you do these exercises again and again.

As we have finished the examples of the first species let us now go on to the next.

Chapter Two

Half Notes against Whole Notes
in Three Parts

A T THIS point you must call to mind both what was prescribed
concerning this species in two part composition and what
was said of the use of the harmonic triad in three part composition of whole notes against whole notes. There is, however, this
to make things easier: in this species of three part composition a half
note may, for the sake of the harmonic triad, occasionally make a
succession of two parallel fifths acceptable—which can be effected
by the skip of the third, e.g.:

FIG. 120

This progression would not be allowed in two part composition. In
three parts, as I have just said, it may be tolerated for the sake of
the harmonic triad. As models I shall give you three examples so
that it will be easier for you to write the others.

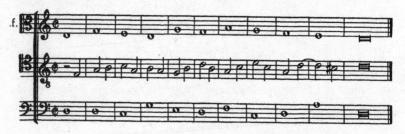

FIG. 121

[1] For. Fig. 121, *eighth bar:* Beethoven (Nottebohm, *Beethoveniana*, I, p. 174) re-

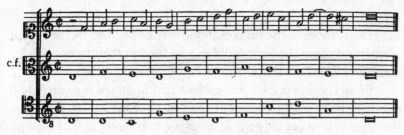

Fig. 122

Fig. 123

Joseph.— I remember that you said some time ago, when you discussed this species in two part composition, that one should never put two half notes following each other on one and the same line,[2] and that therefore ligatures have no place in this species. However, in the final cadences of all three examples I see not only ligatures but, in the final chord of the last example, even a major third—which, as I remember, is no less prohibited.

Aloys.— That is quite so. But since hardly any rule is without exception, I think one must realize when the occasion requires the strict observance of the rule. This is always the case in two part composition; but not in composition of three parts, as you may see clearly from the preceding examples where, in the measures with the liga-

marks: "the downbeat should always have full chords, the upbeat may have scanty ones." (Cf. p. 91.)

[2] From the upbeat to the downbeat.

tures, either a bad unison or an empty sounding octave would have resulted from using plain half notes.[3] That a major third appears in the final chord of the third example may be justified by the cogent reason that there the fifth could not be used in the upper voice because an immediate succession of two fifths would then result.

From these examples it is evident that in one of the voices half notes are to be used throughout the course of the cantus firmus; in the other two voices only whole notes are to be used, so that the half notes are always concordant with the two whole notes. At the same time, good progressions result and the rules are observed as far as possible. Now work out the examples of the remaining modes, setting the cantus firmus by turns in all three voices as I have shown you.

c.f.

FIG. 124

[3] I.c.,   instead of   or

instead of

[4] *For Fig. 124, sixth bar: See p. 54.*

FIG. 125

FIG. 126

FIG. 127

FIG. 128

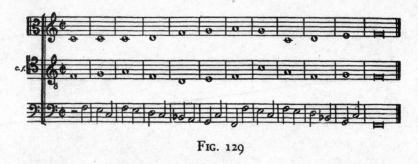

Fig. 129

These examples will be enough for the time being. I shall leave you to work out the three remaining modes in the same way by yourself.

Joseph.— I found this work to be so full of difficulties that it seemed to me in some places nearly impossible to proceed from measure to measure.

Aloys.— I must admit that it is not easy to write in this species, where two half notes must agree well with whole notes of the other voices and everything else be observed that need be observed. However, it becomes most difficult, indeed nearly impossible, if one does not consider one or two measures in advance before deciding to write, as I have already told you. And yet, I can hardly say how useful these exercises are to the student and what ease they will give him in writing. With this training, later on, when the restraints of the cantus firmus are removed, and he is, so to speak, released from his fetters, he will find to his joy that he can write free composition almost as if it were play.

Chapter Three

Quarters against Whole Notes
in Three Parts

SINCE we have to observe the same order here in three part composition that we followed in composition of two parts, it is evident that in this chapter we must deal with the setting of quarters against whole notes. Here, though, one difference is to be noted: the quarters, just as they had to concur with the whole notes of only one other voice in two part composition, have here in three part composition to concur with the whole notes of two other voices. In addition, it is necessary to take into account not only what was said in the corresponding chapter on two part composition, but also everything that has been prescribed so far concerning the species in three part composition.

Joseph.— Does anything else occur in this species that needs special attention?

Aloys.— Nothing, except that, as in all species of counterpoint so in this one, the greatest consideration must be given to the notes that come on the downbeat.

Joseph.— Then I should like to try to write an example of this species without having a model.

Aloys.— Good. But take care whenever you cannot use the harmonic triad on the first quarter occurring on the upbeat, to use it on the second or third quarters.[1]

---

[1] I.e., the second, third, or fourth quarters of the measure.

92

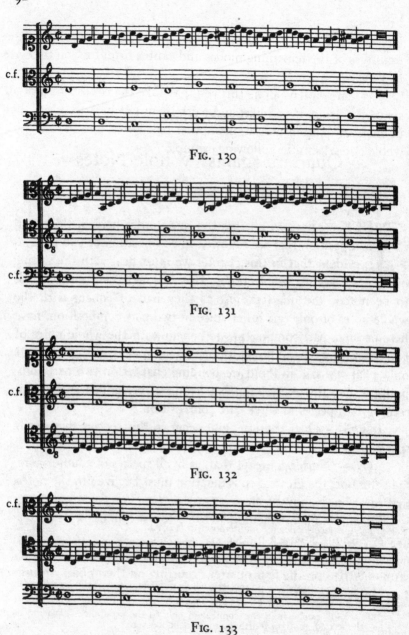

FIG. 130

FIG. 131

FIG. 132

FIG. 133

² For Fig. 132, *tenth bar*: The note g occurs here (and again on p. 123), as a re-
turning or auxiliary note which ordinarily, according to the rules of Fux, and even those

From these examples, which are not inept, I see that you already have a rather good knowledge of this species. Therefore, I shall leave the examples of the remaining modes and cantus firmi for you to study by yourself.

When you have done this you may take the cantus firmi of all six modes again, if you like, and work them out in such a way that in one part quarters are set, in another half notes, and in the third, whole notes, as in the following example:[3]

FIG. 134

I can hardly describe how great the beauty and grace are that are given the composition by this threefold variety of note values. Therefore I should very much like you to work seriously on this exercise, following the threefold or fourfold [5] interchange of the cantus firmus that we have used before.

Joseph.— I shall make the greatest effort to do this, for your advice is always law to me.

Aloys.— Let us now go on to

of Martini (*Esemplare*, p. xxvi.) should be avoided. However, in this particular form—approached from, and returning to, the upper second—it was commonly used in the Palestrina style (see Jeppesen, *Counterpoint*, p. 125).

[3] Here the part in whole notes should, if possible, contain only notes consonant with the cantus firmus (cf. Jeppesen, *Counterpoint*, p. 184, and Bellermann, *Contrapunkt*, p. 213).

[4] *For Fig. 134*: In the second species a whole note may occasionally be used in the next to the last measure. Cf. Figs. 173 and 174.

[5] "Fourfold" can refer in this connection only to the possibility of placing the cantus firmus in any one of the four registers (clefs).

Chapter Four

The Ligature

HERE one has to call to mind what has been said concerning the ligatures in two part composition. The way in which they were used there is not changed in three part composition and should be strictly followed. In addition, it has only to be shown how the concord with the added third voice must be managed. It is important to remember here what has already been said before: that the ligature is nothing but a delaying of the note following. Therefore, even though it seems strange, one has to set the same consonance in the third voice that one would have used if the ligature had been omitted. This is made clear in the following examples:

Without Ligatures

Fig. 135

With Ligatures

Fig. 136

From this it can be seen that the third voice has the same consonances in both examples without the interference of the ligatures. The same thing holds true of ligatures used in the lowest voice, or bass, e.g.:

FIG. 137

If the ligatures were removed for the sake of the harmonic triad—which, however, would be impossible because of another consideration, the immediate succession of several fifths—these measures would appear as follows:

FIG. 138

I am giving you this faulty example, my dear Josephus, in order to show you by it that the nature of consonances is not changed by the ligatures; it remains exactly the same.[1]

---

[1] I.e., in both cases, fifths are involved. However, in one instance the succession of fifths is incorrect and therefore prohibited; in the other, it is permitted. The nature of the consonances employed is not changed, or, in other words, in measures containing dissonant syncopations the essential part is the upbeat, the second, consonant, half.

Joseph.— From this statement, dear master, a doubt occurs to me which I should like to express if you don't mind.

Aloys.— Speak out freely. Your long silence has already made me wonder whether or not you understood everything I said while you did not interrupt me.

Joseph.— If as you said the ligatures do not change anything, both the first example—the one with the ligatures, which you gave a moment ago—and the second must be equally wrong. For, if in the second example, without the ligatures, an immediate succession of several fifths results, the first example, with the ligatures, is for the same reason faulty if the ligatures be disregarded.

Aloys.— I am very pleased by your clever argument which is proof of your keen attention. But aside from the fact that one has to respect the authority of the famous masters skilled in the art, who have approved the first example but disapproved the second, you must know that my statement, "ligatures do not change anything," has reference only to the essential nature of consonances, identical in both examples. Who could deny that in other respects there is great power in ligatures—the ability to avoid or improve incorrect passages?

Joseph.— By this distinction my argument would be dismissed, if it were not for the example of a syncopation that occurred some time ago in two part composition and that you rejected as incorrect, because there the ligature could not make a succession of two octaves acceptable.

Fig. 139

Just as in this example the ligature cannot make the bad succession of two octaves less noticeable, so it will not be able to amend that of the two fifths in the following one:

Fig. 140

Aloys.— In order to dispose of this rather important objection one must realize that much is prohibited in the upper register—being there more perceptible and more obvious to the ear—that may be tolerated in the lower register, because there it becomes somewhat blurred on account of the lowness and does not strike the ear so sharply. For highness accentuates and lowness subdues. However, in order to bring to bear a more fundamental reason, I should like to remind you of what has previously been said about the different perfections of the intervals: the fifth is a perfect consonance, the octave a more perfect one, and the unison the most perfect of all; and the more perfect a consonance, the less harmony it has. In addition, we know that the dissonances in themselves are altogether lacking the grace and charm of harmony; and that whatever pleasantness and beauty they may give the ear have to be attributed to the beauty of the succeeding consonances to which they resolve. From this it is clear that a dissonance which resolves to a fifth will be more acceptable than one which resolves to an octave. Hence, it is not surprising that the great masters consider the first example wrong, the second, however, as conforming to the rules of counterpoint. Finally, a resolution will be regarded more indulgently the closer the perfect consonance to which a dissonance moves is to the nature of an imperfect consonance.[2] Now then, if this explanation is sufficient, go on to the exercises in this species of counterpoint.

Joseph.— I shall do as you say.

[2] Jeppesen, *Counterpoint*, p. 21, quotes Vicentino (*L'antica musica ridotta alla moderna prattica*, 1555) who says with reference to the resolution of a dissonance into a perfect consonance: "Nature is not fond of extremes."

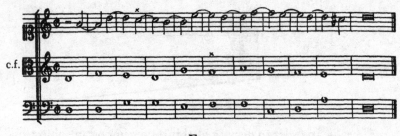

FIG. 141

Aloys.— Why did you mark a mistake or rather an uncertainty in the third measure of the upper voice?

Joseph.— I had not forgotten that the first of the tied notes has always to be consonant. Yet I used a dissonance, the fourth, in this place—for one thing, because I couldn't find any other possibility on account of the necessity of using two half notes in each measure, and for another, because I remembered having seen passages like this in the works of the great masters.

Aloys.— Your uncertainty in this matter is very praiseworthy and shows your keen attention. It doesn't matter, though, if this measure does not follow the rules strictly. If I said that the first note of the ligature must always be consonant, that applies only to the instances in which the lower voice moves from bar to bar, but not to the instances in which the bass remains on a pedal point—as it is usually called—that is, in the same position. In such a case a ligature involving only dissonances is not only correct but even very beautiful, as is shown in the following example: [3]

---

[3] In this case, the distribution of consonances and dissonances is like that in the third species of counterpoint.

Fig. 142

And what does the other mark, in the sixth bar, indicate?

Joseph. — I know that the seventh must be set with the third,[4] but here I have taken the octave since the cantus firmus is not to be changed.

Aloys. — You should remember that we are still dealing with exercises and must try to use a ligature in every single measure. Therefore, in this place, we need not take too much care of the absolute concord with the other voices which we have discussed before, and which we shall also deal with again. In free composition, however, where nothing prevents a dissonance from having its proper concord, this would have to be considered differently. Thus, the seventh combined with the octave should be accepted here. Now to the remaining exercises.

Fig. 143

[4] Cf. Martini, *Esemplare*, p. xxviii. Martini states such rules in greater detail but quotes (*Esemplare*, p. 142) and follows the general principle given at the beginning of this chapter.

FIG. 144

Why did you use a rest for a whole bar in the lower voice at the beginning of the last example?

Joseph. — Since I couldn't find any possibility of using a ligature, and thought that the space should not be filled with another species of counterpoint, I tried to help myself out of the difficulty with a rest.

Aloys. — I am pleased by your caution. However, it could have been done in the following way:

FIG. 145

Here the tenor takes the place of the bass in the first measure—a thing that not only the tenor may do, but also the alto and possibly even the soprano. This part, though, whichever it may be, must be taken as a basis and from it one has to reckon. Now go on to the examples of the next two modes in their natural order.

101

Fig. 146

Fig. 147

Fig. 148

Fig. 149

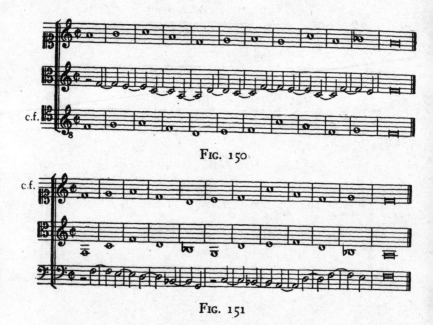

Fig. 150

Fig. 151

Aloys.— As far as the ligatures and the use of two whole notes [6] in every measure permit, these exercises are well worked out according to the rules of harmony, for the restrictions of this species make it impossible to have a harmony perfect in all parts. Besides, as I have already said, more attention should be paid here to the ligatures which make it possible for us to acquire a thorough knowledge of this species, since they occur in these exercises in so many forms. I should like to recommend the ligatures to you, therefore, as one of the chief excellences of composition.

What could still be improved is the first measure of the last example—which stands as follows:

[5] *For Fig. 146, second bar, and Fig. 147, second bar:* See p. 62.
[6] Cf. pp. 121 and 129.

FIG. 152

Here a hidden succession of two fifths between the alto and the soprano parts occurs, which is easily perceptible to the ear and should be avoided in three part composition.[7] This may be managed by using a rest in the alto, as follows:

FIG. 153

Joseph.— I have used a similar remedy in the sixth measure of the bass part of the same exercise, where I couldn't find any other possibility of continuing the series of ligatures.[8]

Aloys.— Well done. The rule to use a ligature in every measure is to be observed only where it is possible. Now go through the three remaining modes in the same way.

[7] In general, hidden successions of fifths and octaves are already permitted in three part writing if the voice leading is otherwise good; see Fig. 100. However, the opening of this example deals with two, rather than three, voices (the second and third parts start on the same tone), and the suspension in the bass makes it doubly evident that the other two voices move in the same direction.

[8] *Marginal note in the original: g could be kept as a syncopation.*

Chapter Five

Florid Counterpoint

WHAT this species is and how it is written you will remember, I suppose, from what has been said about it in two part composition: it is a combination of all five [1] species contrived in as beautiful and singable a way as is possible. How the concord with the two other voices—consisting of whole notes—is to be treated you will know, I think, from the three part exercises which we have done so far. So it does not seem necessary to spend any more time on explanations. Let us go on to the examples without delay.

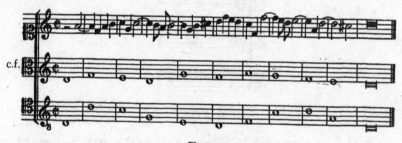

FIG. 154

FIG. 155

[1] Strictly speaking: of all four.

FIG. 156

FIG. 157

FIG. 158

FIG. 159

These examples should be sufficient for the time being. If you will go through the exercises of the four remaining modes by yourself with the same care, you will easily achieve an adequate knowledge of this species. You should keep in mind that oblique motion usually facilitates the work in any single measure. Now to four part composition.

THIRD PART

Chapter One

Four Part Composition or Writing in Four Voices

THAT the complete harmonic triad is already contained in three parts or in composition with three voices has been stated before. Hence it follows that the fourth voice to be added cannot be employed otherwise than by doubling some consonance already present in the three other voices—except for some dissonant chords which are to be discussed in another place. Although there is a great difference between the unison and the octave so far as the interval and the register are concerned, there is none at all in their general designation: for instance the unison and the octave are both called c. The octave is considered a repetition, so to speak, of the unison. Hence, as a rule, a four part chord will consist of a third, fifth, and octave. Wherever one cannot use the octave because of incorrect progressions (which is often the case), one must double the third or, more rarely, the sixth.[1] Moreover, the rules given in the First Book concerning progressions and motion should be followed so far as possible, which holds not only when reckoning from

[1] "Sixth": a misprint for "fifth"? In the original copy, however, there is no such indication, either in the Errata or in the added marginal notes. Even in Beethoven's "Introduction" (Nottebohm, *Beethoveniana*, I, p. 180) we find this paragraph repeated without change. The possibilities mentioned seem to refer only to the chord $\begin{smallmatrix}6\\3\\1\end{smallmatrix}$ which in four parts would be extended to $\begin{smallmatrix}8\\6\\3\\1\end{smallmatrix}$, $\begin{smallmatrix}10\\6\\3\\1\end{smallmatrix}$, or $\begin{smallmatrix}13\\6\\3\\1\end{smallmatrix}$. They do not take into consideration the harmonic triad $\begin{smallmatrix}5\\3\\1\end{smallmatrix}$, which Fux took as a basis and which would normally be mentioned first. At any rate, the possibility of doubling the fifth must be mentioned here.

the bass to the other voices but also from any one voice to any other.

I said: so far as possible. For one is sometimes forced to accept a hidden succession of fifths or octaves on account of the requirements of the melody, or of the imitation,[2] or of the limiting effect of the cantus firmus. However, the less one departs from the general rules, the more perfect a four part composition will be.

Joseph.— This is not yet quite clear to me. I think I may need an example or two in order to understand it better.

Aloys.— The following example will easily clarify any obscurities:

FIG. 160

Do not be surprised that all consonances, even the compound intervals, are designated by simple numerals, unlike the practice followed thus far. I did this only in order that the doubling of the consonances might become plainer to the eye. This model you should follow now, and if there is any doubt remaining in your mind, let me know; if not, start working on this cantus firmus, using it in each voice by turns as you have been doing.

Joseph.— Does it make any difference which consonance one gives to a voice?

---

[2] Only when applying the rules of strict counterpoint to free writing.

Aloys.— Yes, decidedly. I believe you know this already from the three part exercises and from what has just been said. Aside from the fact that any consonance should, if possible, occupy its proper place in the natural order, it is most important to consider whether a correct progression will be possible from the chord of the first measure built up in this way, to the second, third, or even fourth measures. If not, the structure of the first measure will have to be changed, and the consonances will have to be distributed in such a way that there will be the possibility of proceeding easily and correctly to the following measures.

Joseph.— What is this proper place of the consonances, which you have mentioned?

Aloys.— It is the order that results from the harmonic division of the octave.[3] Obviously the fifth is produced first by this division; and by a further division of the fifth, the third is produced. This order should be observed when placing the consonances, except when some special reason—usually the progression to the following measures—is against it. Let me give you an example showing the natural order of the consonances:

Fig. 161

You see, firstly, the fifth resulting from the harmonic division of the octave; secondly, the octave that we had taken as the basis; and thirdly, the third or rather tenth, which results from the division of the fifth.

Joseph.— According to the construction of our modern keyboard it seems that the third should occupy the first place—before the fifth, and therefore a four part chord should be built up in this manner:

[3] See p. 142, Appendix.

FIG. 162

Aloys.— It seems so, yet actually this is not the case. The order
is to be decided upon according to the natural division, not according to the construction of the keyboard. Moreover, the third placed
in the low register and so close to the bass results in a dull and in-
distinct sound. The greater the proportional numbers that determine
an interval, the brighter the sound of this interval, the higher therefore, too, the register that it requires. The proportional numbers
of the fifth are 2 and 3 which equal 5. Those of the third, 4 and 5
which equal 9. From this it is clear that according to the natural order
the fifth should be used in the lower register, the third in the upper.
Go on, now, if there is no further doubt in your mind, and do the
remaining work in this and in the other modes. Consider the prob-
lems of every measure carefully, comparing the single parts one with
another, so that nothing contrary to the rules can creep in. In order
to achieve this, close attention is needed, and one has to take care
that not only the bass—or lowest part—and the other voices concur
according to the rules, but also the inner voices with one another.

Joseph.— From the preceding four part example I see that the
interval of the fourth which you said is a dissonance and therefore
prohibited in the composition of note against note occurs sometimes
between the inner voices. I could not pass this without a question.

Aloys.— You are right. However, one must remember that
the *nature* of the intervals, whether they are consonant or dissonant,
is to be determined by reckoning from the bass regardless of what
may occur between the inner voices, if only mistakes such as successions of two fifths or two octaves are avoided.[4] As for the rest, one
has to observe that the closer the parts are led together the more
perfect the sound will be, for: a power compressed will become
stronger. If you run into difficulties, as can hardly be avoided, under-

---

[4] This already holds in three part writing; cf. p. 71.

stand that the way to perfection is through hardship. Without an
adversary one cannot be victorious, and for the contest one must arm
oneself with unflagging zeal and steadfastness and patience.

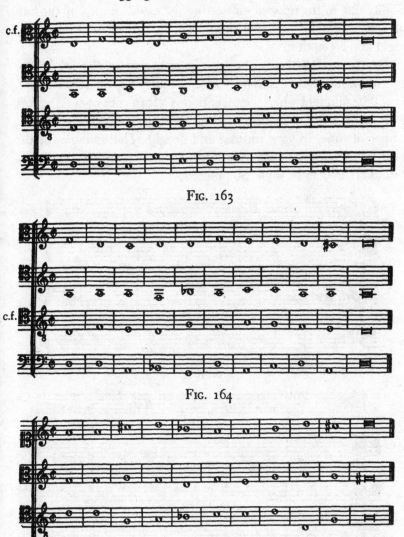

FIG. 163

FIG. 164

FIG. 165

Joseph.— With some hesitation I have led the tenor—in spite of your warning—so close to the bass that the thirds occur mostly in the lower register. I did so because I could not find any other possibility due to the necessity of setting the cantus firmus by turns in all four voices. Therefore, I should like to submit it to your judgment and correction.

Aloys.— It is true; since one is restricted to the use of the cantus firmus, these examples, written as exercises, cannot be better. It will be different when the invention is left to your own taste. Just how useful these exercises are to the student, you will learn in the course of time, to your surprise and delight. The examples of the next two modes with the usual fourfold interchange of the cantus firmus are now to be done. So proceed:

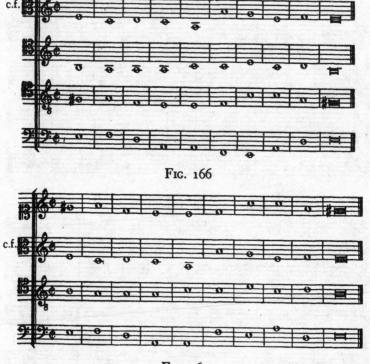

FIG. 166

FIG. 167

Fig. 168

Fig. 169

Fig. 170

116

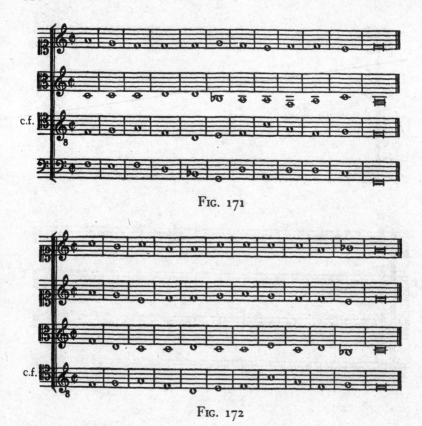

Fig. 171

Fig. 172

However well these examples are written the inflexibility of the cantus firmus will not allow such a composition to be worked out strictly according to the rules of motion and progression—which could be done easily in free composition. The examples of the three remaining modes are to be done in the same way, with the cantus firmus appearing by turns in all four voices.

Chapter Two

Half Notes against Whole Notes

HERE you must recall what has been said previously, in three part composition, concerning this species of counterpoint. All this must be kept in mind when composing in four parts, and there is no difference except that there the two half notes must agree with two whole notes; here, however, with three. For the rest, one should observe what has been said about four part composition of note against note, as far, though, as the restricted nature of this species permits. Now go on to the exercises.

FIG. 173

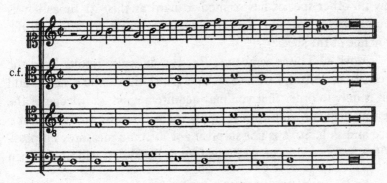

FIG. 174

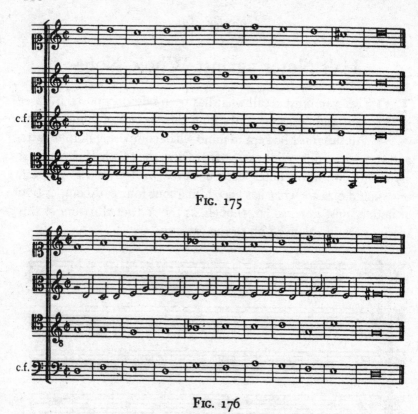

Fig. 175

Fig. 176

Joseph.— I find this species of counterpoint very difficult; until now no other species has seemed so hard as this. At times it was impossible to write the next to the last measure according to the principle of the species.

Aloys.— This is very true. But the difficulty results from the necessity of setting two half notes against three whole notes; and this is only in order that you may acquire a good knowledge of the consonances and will learn to apply them carefully and with assurance and skill. So it is not surprising if in some measures no possibility of proceeding can easily be found. Besides, it will not happen

[1] For Fig. 174, *eighth bar:* Cf. Fig. 42.

in any kind of free composition that a series of measures will have to be worked out in this manner. These lessons are not worked out for actual use but for exercise. If one knows how to read one need no longer bother with spelling; similarly, the species of counterpoint are given only for purposes of study. The exercises in the remaining modes I leave for you to work out at home.

Chapter Three

Quarters against Whole Notes

T HE requirements of this species may be recalled from what has been said about it in two and three part composition. Nothing else need be added, except that the concords are to be dealt with differently. Just as the concords had to be managed with one whole note in two part composition, and with two whole notes in three part composition, so now in four part composition the four quarters must be concordant with three whole notes according to the principles of harmony which you already know. The examples will make this clearer:

c.f.

B.

A.

Fig. 177

Joseph.— Why—if I may ask, dear master—have you doubled the third in the fourth measure? I think one could have used a unison instead of the third in the tenor, in this way:

FIG. 178

Aloys. — Certainly it could have been done in this way. However, aside from the fact that a unison on the downbeat detracts considerably from the complete harmony of the composition, it has also to be taken into account that the third, or rather the tenth, which occurs only in passing in the upper voice, would be too weak since it is not heard continuously. What doubt does the second sign, B, indicate?

Joseph. — The progression between the alto and the tenor parts seems to be wrong because it occurs from one perfect consonance to another by direct motion.

Aloys. — I will say that this progression could not be managed otherwise because one must necessarily use whole notes, and therefore it may be tolerated. It could easily be improved if the whole note in the tenor could be divided thus:

Fig. 179

This holds also for the examples of the previous species in which there are many places that would be considered faulty if it were not for the necessity of using whole notes. Now go on to the remaining exercises, always changing the position of the cantus firmus.

Fig. 180

With this example, my dear Josephus, you have given proof of the remarkable progress that you have made, and that of all things that have been explained in the course of so many lessons nothing has escaped your memory. For you have always used a complete harmonic triad on the first quarter, and from there you have had the three remaining quarters move in such a way that the following measure was approached simply. Moreover, you have correctly observed the rules of harmony and of the different species by provid-

ing a full harmonic triad, namely, a third and a fifth, on the downbeat
or beginning of each measure. Continue.

FIG. 181

What does the letter A mean in the second measure of the
upper voice?

Joseph.— I have some doubt about the progression from one
perfect consonance to another by similar motion; that is, from the
octave to the fifth, the more so since it occurs in the outer voices.

Aloys.— I said a short while ago, and should like to repeat
here, that one must admit such progressions sometimes because of
the necessity of writing whole notes, especially as, even in free composition, they cannot always be avoided; though they are to be tolerated in the inner voices rather than in the outer voices, as you have
rightly remarked.

FIG. 182

[1] For Fig. 182, tenth bar: Cf. Fig. 132.

Joseph.— The letter A in the tenor marks a lapse from the general rule again, because of the reason just mentioned; for there is a progression from an imperfect to a perfect consonance, that is, from a third to a fifth by direct motion, which I think may be tolerated here because of the same necessity.

Aloys.— You are right. Evidently it cannot be done better so long as there are the limitations of this species. The defect is harder to notice in this instance, though, because it occurs in the inner voices. The next mode, E (*la, mi*),[2] you should work out in the same way now in my presence, since it is the most difficult of all due to the absence of the one perfect fifth. The others I leave you to do at home.

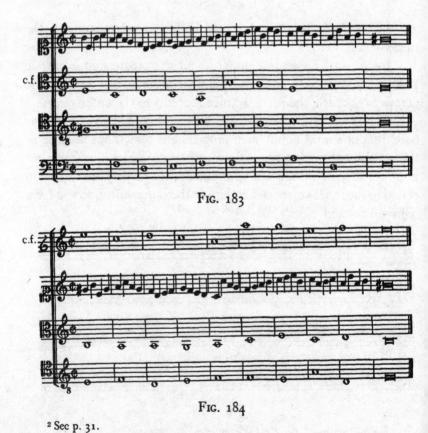

Fig. 183

Fig. 184

[2] See p. 31.

FIG. 185

FIG. 186

Joseph.— Between the parts written in the soprano and violin clefs, from the first measure to the second, there is a progression from a third to a fifth which is contrary to the rule usually observed. But for the reasons mentioned before I neither wished nor was able to improve it.

Aloys.— As I have said already, one must concede much to a necessity here which otherwise in free composition would have to be avoided. So also the progression at B which occurs with respect to the lowest voice from an octave to a fifth in direct motion need not be considered a mistake because of the difficulty of this species.[3]

---

[3] Cf. Beethoven (Nottebohm, *Beethoveniana*, I, p. 174): "Such liberties are more acceptable in a descending than in an ascending motion." However, in his *Intro-*

The remaining modes, then, you may work out at home. We shall proceed now to the next species.

duction (*ibid*, p. 181), we find Beethoven's comment on this example and this particular instance (the succession occurring between the outer voices): "The second progression, at B, would never be excusable for my ear."

Chapter Four

The Ligature

WE have finished the species involving quarter notes. The ligatures will now follow, as is evident from the two and three part exercises, and I assume that you know what these are. It only remains to be explained which concords the ligatures should be accompanied by in four part composition. Concerning this something has already been said in three part composition, that is, they call for those consonances which would also be used if the ligatures were removed. The reason for this has been given, too, in the same place: the ligature is nothing but a delaying of the note following. As to the consonances, however, this does not alter anything. The examples will make this clear.

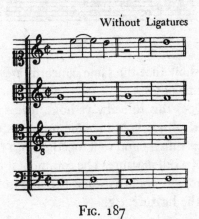

Without Ligatures

FIG. 187

FIG. 188

FIG. 189

These examples show that the same concords are used for the tied notes as for the free notes.

Joseph.— Does this rule always hold, revered master?

Aloys.— It does not hold in some instances of this species in which the ligatures must sound well together with three whole notes for the duration of a full measure. The commonest instance in which this cannot be brought about is when the seventh is used together with the fifth in the ligature, e.g.:

FIG. 190

If the ligature were removed, a dissonance with the tenor would result which is faulty and decidedly to be avoided.

Joseph.— What can one do in this case?

Aloys.— One must divide the whole note in the tenor part, thus:

FIG. 191

Joseph.— But in this species division of the whole note is not permitted.

Aloys.— Right—when dividing it can possibly be avoided. However, a number of cases will occur, as you will soon learn from the examples to come, wherein one cannot help making a division.

Therefore the rule that one must write three whole notes cannot be so strictly observed in this species.

Joseph.— If the seventh is heard with the octave, the whole note need not be divided at all, as I see from your last example.

FIG. 192

Aloys.— That applies only in this case though, where nothing prevents the octave's being used instead of the fifth. Still, you will frequently find instances where, on account of a series of preceding or following notes, the octave cannot be employed and the fifth must necessarily be used. Then, and in many other cases, the whole note must be divided as the following examples show: [1]

FIG. 193

[1] Cf. Martini, *Esemplare*, p. 11, and Mozart, *Fundamente des General-Basses*, p. 8, where this way of accompanying a tie ⎕ is given preference over ⎕

Joseph.— There is nothing that is unclear to me in this example except for the progression from the fourth measure to the fifth between the tenor and the alto parts.

FIG. 194

Aloys.— In order that you may have no misgivings concerning this progression you must know that the interval of the fourth in the inner voices is not very prominent; in fact, it rather assumes the character of an imperfect consonance. Therefore, this progression is to be regarded just as though it occurred from a perfect consonance to an imperfect consonance in direct motion, a principle which ought to be well considered.

Now to the remaining examples.

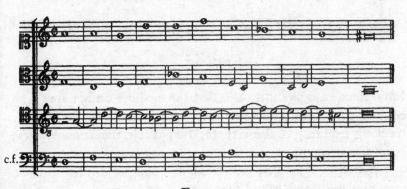

FIG. 195

Fig. 196

Fig. 197

From these examples it is plain that the ligatures cannot always be coupled with three undivided whole notes (as this species, strictly speaking, requires); or else, if that is still possible, they cannot always result in a harmony perfect according to all rules.

Joseph.— I see that several whole notes are divided in these examples and I understand the reason. But I cannot find that the harmony is, as you said, imperfect in any place.

Aloys.— Don't you see that in the first example, on the downbeat of the sixth measure, the fifth which is necessary for a complete harmony is missing? Furthermore, in the fifth measure of the last example the second is doubled while the sixth which is required for an absolutely perfect harmony is missing—as the following example shows:

FIG. 198

Finally, in the sixth measure of the same example the fourth is doubled, although as a rule one doubles the second rather than the fourth.

Joseph.— Why should one double the second rather than the fourth?

Aloys.— It is not so much a matter of the second or the fourth as it is a matter of the complete harmony.[3] As a complete harmonic chord consists of a combination of third, fifth, and octave, whereas in the example mentioned there is a doubled fifth instead of the octave, it is evident that the harmony is not perfect. Here, though, I am not referring to the first part of the measure where the second occurs—for this under no circumstances allows the presence of the octave—but to the second part of the measure where the octave is lacking. As an example:

2 *For Fig. 198:* Cf. footnote on p. 130.

3 I.e., the resolution which follows from the doubling of the second or fourth, respectively, on the upbeat. Nottebohm (*Beethovens Studien*, pp. 37, 42) stresses the fact that Haydn followed Fux's and Martini's rules concerning the resolution of dissonant syncopations with great care—not only in correcting Beethoven's exercises, but also in his own works.

FIG. 199

Such slight lapses from the strict perfection of this species are to be allowed because of the great benefit which these exercises afford the student; for they teach him not only how to write a composition but also how one may depart occasionally—if need be—from the strict rules.

I have given you here models of this species and I leave it to you to work out the remaining five modes in like manner, using the cantus firmus, as before, by turns in all four voices.

Now let us proceed to the fifth species.

Chapter Five

Florid Counterpoint

THIS species as you know, my dear Josephus, deals with florid counterpoint. What it is and how it is written I suppose you remember from the previous examples and explanations, especially from the exercises in this species in three part composition. So nothing new need be added here, except that the fourth voice must also be in whole notes and must be worked in according to the principles of four part composition.

Now to the examples.

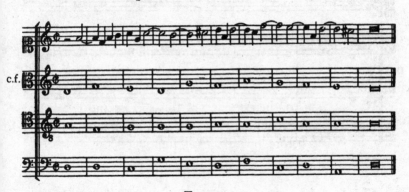

Fig. 200

Fig. 201

FIG. 202

FIG. 203

Joseph.— I see that, as in the ligature species, so here too, several whole notes are divided.

Aloys.— When I say that the whole notes must remain undivided, I mean wherever this is possible. However, you will notice that where there was an opportunity the rule was strictly observed. The exercises in the five remaining modes, you may go through in the same manner.

As we have now completed the five species singly, I want to urge you to write them also in combination. Keeping the same cantus firmus you may combine, for example, half notes, quarters, and liga-

---

[1] For Fig. 200, second bar, and Fig. 201, second bar: See p. 62.

tures. Thus each part will have its own characteristic motion, and the whole composition will possess a wonderful variety. As an example:

FIG. 204

In the same way I want you to work out this and the five remaining modes and to use the fourfold interchange of the position of the cantus firmus so that it will appear in each of the four voices. In doing this you should make an effort to take into account at once what has been said about each species separately and to observe strictly what applies to the voices in their relation to each other—all of which I believe is now familiar to you. How great a profit these exercises, if done properly, will give the student is not easily expressed, especially as hardly any difficulty will arise which will not be known to you from your work in the different species. So, if you wish to make progress in this art, I want to advise you earnestly to devote considerable time to the practice of these five species. You should try always to find new cantus firmi for yourself; and set yourself a period of at least a year or two in which to apply yourself to this study. Do not allow yourself to be seduced into proceeding too early to your own free compositions. In your pleasure over them you would spend your time roving here and there, but never achieve real mastery.

Joseph.— The road you bid me take, revered master, is rough and thorny. It is hardly possible to spend so much time on such a difficult task without becoming tired of it.

Aloys.— I can understand your complaint, my dear Josephus, and I sympathize with you. But the mountain of the muses is to be reached only by a very precipitous path. There is no craft—however modest it may be—to which the novice does not have to serve an apprenticeship of at least three years. What should I say then about music, which not only surpasses the simpler crafts and arts in ingenuity, difficulty and richness, but, in fact cannot be rivaled by any of the liberal arts? The benefits your efforts may bring you; the hope of success; the facility in writing which you will gradually acquire; and finally, the firm confidence that what you are writing is well written, may encourage you.

*   *   *

Joseph.— It seems, venerated master, that you want to put an end to the work.

Aloys.— Yes. Have you not noticed how weakness and torpor, the usual forewarnings of my old enemy, the gout, are stealing over me? Besides, you know that because of my age and my almost ceaseless ill-health I have already become so weak that if the malady attacks me with its usual violence and lasts, as it generally does, six months, I have every reason to fear that this time I cannot escape. In order, therefore, that the lack of an end may not be added to the imperfections of this little work, I shall conclude it now.

Joseph.— Then you will not say anything concerning composition in more than four voices?

Aloys.— I had indeed intended to add to this work a chapter on composition for more than four parts. Since, however, I am interrupted by ill-health as you see, and confined to my bed, I can only continue later and write a special study of this, if Almighty God chooses to give me further life and renewed strength. With the help of this study you may then learn everything you will still need to know, even without your teacher's instruction. However, understand that to him who masters four part composition the way to composition with more voices is already made quite clear; for as the number of voices increases, the rules are to be less rigorously observed.

Farewell, and pray to God for me.

Appendix

The species of the harmonic and arithmetical divisions are used by Fux in the theoretical part of the *Gradus ad Parnassum* (First Book) for deriving a number of intervals from the basic interval of the octave. The order in which they are thus found is referred to in determining their different importance. This procedure may seem complicated as compared to the modern way of using the evidences of the series of overtones. However, since it may be important for the understanding of Fux's text, I should like to render briefly some parts of the First Book dealing with these mathematical operations.

Fux uses two progressive proportions, the arithmetical proportion 4:3:2, and the harmonic proportion 6:4:3. The harmonic division (not the "golden mean") is a species no longer in use today. It is based on the principle: the components of the progressive proportion a:b:c correspond to the components of the harmonic series if

$$\frac{1}{c} - \frac{1}{b} = \frac{1}{b} - \frac{1}{a} \ (= n).$$

The arithmetical series, however, is based on the principle: the components of the progressive proportion a:b:c correspond to the components of an arithmetical series if

$$c - b = b - a \ (= n).$$

In the arithmetical series, accordingly, the remainders of the values are constant, in the harmonic series the remainders of the reciprocal values are constant. Fux, in the chapter dealing with the harmonic division, shows one way to find a harmonic proportion from an arithmetical proportion. In the arithmetical proportion 4:3:2 the two outer components are to be multiplied by the inner component; i.e., $4 \times 3 = 12$

and $3 \times 2 = 6$. The products represent the outer components of a harmonic proportion. In order to find the proper middle component the outer components of the arithmetical proportion have to be multiplied: $4 \times 2 = 8$. Thus we find the harmonic proportion 12:8:6. In other words, from the arithmetical proportion a:b:c we have found the harmonic proportion $a_1:b_1:c_1 = ab:ac:bc$.

In defining the consonant and the dissonant fourths, Fux derives the interval of the fourth twice from the ratio of the octave 2:1 (the greater number indicating the lower tone according to the divisions of the string on the monochord). This proportion is first arithmetically and then harmonically divided. In the first instance, the proportion 2:1 is extended to 4:2, and by inserting the middle component 3 the arithmetical proportion 4:3:2 is completed. Translating the proportions into musical intervals we find

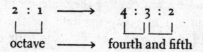

In the second instance, the proportion 2:1 is extended to 6:3, and by inserting the middle component 4 the harmonic proportion 6:4:3 is completed:

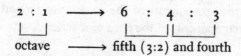

Fux uses the harmonic division again in explaining the "natural order" of the consonances (octave—fifth—major third; an evolution which can be observed, for instance, in the closing chords of the old many-voiced music; cf. p. 80). The ratio of the octave, 2:1, is once more taken as a basis. This proportion is harmonically divided, and the first new proportion resulting is again harmonically divided. Thus the development from the simplest to the more complicated natural intervals is shown by the harmonic division. As before, the proportion 2:1 is extended to 6:3 and harmonically divided by the middle component 4. Of the two intervals represented in the proportion 6:4:3 we choose the first, the interval of the fifth, and apply the harmonic division to its ratio 3:2. The proportion has to be extended to 15:10 and the middle component 12 (which can be found according to the formula for the harmonic series mentioned before) is inserted. The result is

$$3:2 \longrightarrow \quad 15 \qquad : \qquad 12 \qquad : \qquad 10$$

fifth $\longrightarrow$ major third ($5:4$) and minor third ($6:5$)

In the natural order, illustrated through the harmonic division, we have found the major third as the next interval.

All these computations are based upon mensurations on the monochord. Today we may find a clearer and more valid explanation of the interval relations in the ordinal numbers of the series of overtones:

$$\begin{array}{cccccc} 1 & 2 & 3 & 4 & 5 & 6 \\ C & c & g & c' & e' & g' \end{array}$$

Here, however, all proportions are reversed, since the number of vibrations, instead of the divisions of the string, are taken as a basis, the number of vibrations and the respective divisions of the string being inversely proportional. Therefore, in the ordinal numbers of the series of overtones we also find the "natural order" represented by the components of an arithmetical, and no longer of a harmonic, series, since the formulas underlying the structure of these series use reciprocal values in corresponding places.

Notes

*concerning the original text, the changes made in it,
and passages freely translated.*

THE COMPLETE title of the work reads:

*Gradus ad Parnassum, Sive Manductio ad Compositionem Musicæ
regularem, Methodo novâ, ac certâ, nondum antè tam exacto ordine in
lucem edita: Elaborata à Joanne Josepho Fux, Sacræ Cæsareæ, ac Regiæ
Catholicæ Majestatis Caroli VI. Romanorum Imperatoris supremo
chori praefecto. Viennæ Austriæ, Typis Joannis Petri Van Ghelen, Sac.
Cæs. Regiæque Catholicæ Majestatis Aulæ-Typographi,* 1725.

It is printed in folio, the musical examples being hand-set, and contains 280 numbered pages and 6 unnumbered pages. In some copies a
frontispiece appears preceding the title page. The present translation
covers pages 41 through 139, page 279, and the preface (three unnumbered pages). The title, Gradus ad Parnassum—first appearing in 1687
for a dictionary of Latin versification—was often used at that time for
treatises dealing with the various arts.

Language and orthography show the usual deviations of ecclesiasti-
cal from classical Latin. Capitals are generally employed according to
their use in German. There is a distinction made between ſ and s and
between *i* and *j*. For the word *et* the symbol *&* is always used. The
original punctuation has often been changed in the translation for the
sake of greater clarity. Fux has marked the text by using three indicative
symbols—which proved to be of considerable help in the work of translation: ^ for long syllables (notâ-nota), ` for adverbs, conjunctions, and
prepositions, in order to distinguish identical forms with different meanings (versùs-versus), and ' in order to divide words with independent meanings which appear as one word (itáque-itaque). In the musical
examples, we find the note shapes of the old mensural notation, then
still employed in print. According to our modern use, the G clef has
been substituted for the C clefs—though this notation will always be
bound to remain a substitute as compared to the old notation. Acci-

dentals occurring above the staves are not in the original. Ties across a bar line, indicated in the original by a dot in the new measure, have been written out.

Insignificant misprints, missing bar and double-bar lines, and misprints which are listed in the original under "Errata" have been corrected without mention. In one of the original copies which I used for the translation, marginal notes in Latin have been added by an anonymous reader apparently soon after the publication of the work. A number of these, giving interesting comments or correcting misprints, I have adopted.

The choice of freely translated passages listed below has been limited to instances in which musical terms and related references are concerned. Bracketed parts of the Latin text have been omitted in the translation; bracketed parts of the English text have been added. Versions representing free translations which occur several times are always listed in the first instance only.

Page 17, *line* 10 The theory of music: Musica speculativa. In this distinction of theory and practice, I have not used the term "theory of music" in its modern meaning which would comprise *musica speculativa* and *musica activa*. The term "theory of music" whenever used here refers to the material of the First Book, which is not included in this translation.

       ibid. The practice of writing music: Musica activa.

Page 18, *line* 14 Ubi per Aloysium, Magistrum, clarissimum illud Musicae lumen Praenestinum, vel ùt alii volunt, Praeestinum intellego.

Page 20, *line* 11 De Intervallis, Consonantiarum Dissonantiarumque divisione.

      line 19 1. 3. 5. 6. 8. cum suis compositis.

      line 23 Diminished fifth: Quinta falsa.

Page 21, *line* 6 Motus *musicus* est ille ambitus, quo de uno intervallo ad aliud versùs partem auctem, vel gravem fit progressio.

Page 22, *line* 20 Laymen: Musicae Artis expertium.

Page 23, line 5 Complures Contrapunctum [tanquam Genus] continet Species.

Page 27, line 7 Whole note: Nota semibrevis. For the terms of the old mensural notation I have substituted the modern terms in the translation.

Page 28, line 27 Cùm autem Consonantiae imperfectae, & perfectionis expertes sint, & finem concludere non possint.

Page 29, line 1 Ad speciem hujus Contrapuncti.

line 5 In clave Cantûs (descant).

line 16 Notarum numerationem. Fux applies the term "nota" to pairs of notes; later, in three and four parts, to groups of three and four notes. In these cases, I have translated "nota" by "pair of notes," "bar," etc.

Page 30, line 29 In the alto clef: in alto.

line 30 Infra pone Tenorem pro parte Contrapuncti.

Page 33, line 14 Nec adeò tonum constituere potest.

Page 34, line 4 Ex Quinta falsa effici Quinta consonans, adjugendo vel Notae inferiori ♭., vel superiori Diesin ♯.

line 14 Melodic line: modulandi ratio.

Page 36, line 8 Nunc posito Basso infrà Cantum firmum, in eo formetur Contrapunctum.

Page 37, line 10 Where: in quo Compositionis genere.

Fig. 16 In the original, the first note in the upper part appears as *b*, corrected in manuscript.

Page 38, line 13 More [than two] voices: plurium vocum.

Page 39, line 5 Illud in prima Contrapuncti Nota positum N.B.

ibid. Nonnihil adversam relationem efficeret.

line 19 *f♯*: F. Diesi adjunctâ.

Page 42, line 17 "Consonantia imperfecta ad imperfectam"; obviously a misprint.

Page 43, line 2 Neque duas Quintas, neque duas Octavas salvare.

line 9 Those measures: Hypotheses illas.

line 12 De prima Nota ad secundam.

Page 45, Fig. 33 In the original, the sixth note in the upper voice appears as *c*, corrected in manuscript.

line 3 Antequàm autem hanc ipsam Lectionem cum Contrapuncto in inferiori parte componendam aggrediaris.

Page 47, *Fig.* 42 The change of cantus firmus as in the original.

Page 50, *line* 11 In the original, "Consonans," corrected in manuscript.

Page 51, *line* 3 The third note, the dissonance [in the previous examples], is nothing but . . . : tertiam illam Notam, nempe dissonantiam aliud non esse, quàm . . .

Page 57, *Fig.* 67 In the original, the figure 8 appears in the first measure, corrected in manuscript.

Page 60, *line* 16 Quo casu tactus ille Minimis solutis implendus erit.

  line 22 Note: Ligaturam. Probably "notam" is meant and "Ligaturam" an error.

Page 65, *Fig.* 85 In the original, the tie to the last bar in the lower voice is missing.

Page 66, *Fig.* 88 The change of cantus firmus as in the original.

Page 71, *line* 11 Rei gravitas [tenuitatem opprimens].

  line 19 Three whole notes . . . [the upper two] being consonant [with the lowest]: tribus semibrevibus, merisque Consonantiis.

Page 74, *line* 6 Quod verò tantùm intelligendum est.

Page 75, *line* 15 Illud alio modo fieri potuisse demonstras.

Page 76, *line* 5 In parte Tenoris respectu Alti.

Page 77, *line* 9 Non obstante Tertiâ.

Page 78, *Fig.* 101 In the original, the last note in the bass appears as *e*.

Page 79, *line* 1 Esset quidem provisum illi inconvenienti [per motum contrarium].

Page 80, *line* 2 And thus: sive.

  line 16 Don't you realize: [aeque] nihil ad rem.

Page 85, *line* 1 Reliqua tonorum exempla.

Page 88, *line* 12 Observatâ triplici mutatione à me monstratâ.

Page 91, *line* 1 There is no heading for this chapter in the original.

Page 94, *line* 9 Consonance: concordantiam.

Page 98, *line* 3 The first of the tied notes: primam Ligaturae partem.

  line 14 On a pedal point: in mansione.

Page 99, *line* 5 In lectionibus versari, & in studio, . . . inserendi.

  line 7 Non admodum rigori caeterarum concordantiarum inhaerentes.

Page 102, *line* 6 Perfectam sui conficiendi cognitionem exhibent.

  line 10 Of the [last] example: exercitii.

Page 110, *line* 5   The limiting effect of the cantus firmus: subjecti rigor.

Page 111, *line* 21   That we had taken as the basis: per se existentem.

Page 112, *line* 20   In the composition of note against note: in Compositione meris semibrevibus constante.

line 28   Juxta illud: Vis unita fortior.

Page 120, *line* 3   Praeter Concordantiae disparitatem.

Page 123, *Fig.* 181   In the original the seventh note in the bass appears as *a*. However, immediately before, on the preceding page, *f* is indicated by a custos.

line 6   In the original, "de Quinta ad Octavam," corrected in manuscript.

Page 124, *Fig.* 184   In the original, the second note of the seventh bar in the second voice appears as *b*, corrected in manuscript.

Page 127, *line* 1   There is no heading for this chapter in the original.

Page 129, *line* 8   When dividing it can possibly be avoided: Ubi fieri potest.

Page 133, *line* 3   In the original, "quinto," corrected in manuscript.

Page 134, *line* 9   Fifth species: quinta species [hujus Studii] (of counterpoint).

Page 135, *line* 1   There is no heading for this chapter in the original.

Bibliography

Albrechtsberger, Johann Georg
Gründliche Anweisung zur Komposition, Breitkopf, Leipzig, 1790.
Revised edition in *J. G. Albrechtsbergers sämtliche Schriften* by Ignaz Ritter von Seyfried, 3 vols., Tobias Haslinger, Vienna, 1826, 2nd edition 1837 (English translations 1834, 1842, 1855).

Beldemandis, Prosdocimus de
Tractatus de contrapuncto, 1412; published in Edmond de Coussemaker, *Scriptorum de musica medii aevi nova series*, facs. ed., Milan, 1931, Vol. III.

Bellermann, Heinrich
Der Contrapunkt, Julius Springer, Berlin, 1862, 4th edition 1901.

Fux, Johann Joseph
Gradus ad Parnassum, see Notes, p. 144.
Gradus ad Parnassum; oder, Anführung zur regelmässigen musikalischen Composition, translated by Lorenz Mizler, Mizler, Leipzig, 1742.
Salita al Parnasso, translated by Alessandro Manfredi, Carmignani, Carpi, 1761.
Traité de Composition Musicale, translated by Pietro Denis, H. Nadermann, Paris, 1773(?).
Practical Rules for Learning Composition, J. Preston, London, 1791.
Die Lehre vom Kontrapunkt, translated and edited by Alfred Mann, Hermann Moeck, Celle, 1938, 2nd edition 1951.
Steps to Parnassus: The Study of Counterpoint, translated and edited by Alfred Mann with the collaboration of John St. Edmunds, W. W. Norton, New York, 1943 (J. M. Dent & Sons, London, 1944).

Garlandia, Johannes de

Optima introductio in contrapunctum, published in Coussemaker, *Scriptorum* . . . , Vol. III.

Griesinger, Georg August

Biographische Notizen über Joseph Haydn, Breitkopf & Härtel, Leipzig, 1810.

English translation by Vernon Gotwals in *Joseph Haydn, Eighteenth-Century Gentleman and Genius*, University of Wisconsin Press, Madison, Wisc., 1963.

Jeppesen, Knud

Counterpoint, translated by Glen Haydon, Prentice-Hall Inc., New York, 1939.

Das Sprunggesetz des Palestrinastils bei betonten Viertelnoten, in *Kongressbericht*, Basel, 1925, Breitkopf & Härtel, Leipzig.

Mann, Alfred

The Study of Fugue, Rutgers University Press, New Brunswick, N.J., 1958 (Faber and Faber, London, 1959).

Mattheson, Johann

Grosse General-Bass-Schule, Christian Kissner, Hamburg, 1731.

Martini, Padre Giambattista

Esemplare o sia Saggio Fondamentale Pratico di Contrappunto sopra il Canto Fermo, Lelio dalla Volpe, Bologna, 1774.

Monteverdi, Claudio

Il quinto libro de' madrigali, Foreword, Venice, 1607; Facs. ed. in *Tutte le opere di Claudio Monteverdi*, edited by Francesco Malipiero, Universal Edition, Vienna, 1926–42, Vol. X.

English translation in Oliver Strunk, *Source Readings in Music History*, W. W. Norton, New York, 1950.

Mozart, Wolfgang Amadeus

Fundamente des General-Basses, edited by J. G. Siegmeyer, Schneppelsche Buchhandlung, Berlin, 1822.

Thomas Attwoods Theorie- und Kompositionsstudien bei Mozart (*Neue Mozart-Ausgabe, Serie X, Supplement, Werkgruppe* 30). Submitted by Cecil B. Oldman and Erich Hertzmann, edition completed by Daniel Heartz and Alfred Mann, Bärenreiter, Kassel, 1965.

Muris, Johannes de
  Ars contrapunti, published in Coussemaker, *Scriptorum* . . . , Vol. III.
Nottebohm, Gustav
  Beethoveniana, C. F. Peters, Leipzig, 1872.
  Beethoven's Studien. Erster Band. Beethoven's Unterricht bei J. Haydn, Albrechtsberger und Salieri, J. Rieter-Biedermann, Leipzig and Winterthur, 1873.
Plath, Wolfgang
  Beiträge zur Mozart-Autographie I, in *Mozart-Jahrbuch 1960–1961*, Internationale Stiftung Mozarteum, Salzburg, 1961.
Pohl, Carl Ferdinand
  Joseph Haydn, Breitkopf & Härtel, Leipzig, 1878.
Rameau, Jean-Philippe
  Traité de l'harmonie, Ballard, Paris, 1722.
  Nouveau Systême de musique théorique, Ballard, Paris, 1726.
  Génération harmonique, Prault fils, Paris, 1737.
  Démonstration du principe de l'harmonie, Durand & Pissot, Paris, 1750.
Roth, Herman
  Elemente der Stimmführung, Vol. 1, Carl Grüninger Nachf. Ernst Klett, Stuttgart, 1926.
Seyfried, Ignaz Ritter von
  Ludwig van Beethovens Studien, Tobias Haslinger, Vienna, 1832.
  Beethoven Études, translated by François Joseph Fétis, Maurice Schlesinger, Paris, 1833.
  Beethoven's Studies, translated by Henry Hugh Pierson (Edgar Mansfeldt), Schuberth & Co., Leipzig, 1853.
Spitta, Philipp
  Johann Sebastian Bach, translated by Clara Bell and J. A. Fuller Maitland, Novello & Co., London, 1899.
Tinctoris, Johannes
  Diffinitorium musicae, c. 1475;
  Liber de arte contrapuncti, 1477; published in Coussemaker, *Scriptorum* . . . , Vol. IV.

Vicentino, Don Nicola
  L'antica musica ridotta alla moderna prattica, A. Barre, Rome, 1555.
  Facs. ed. by E. E. Lowinsky in *Documenta Musicologica* XVII,
    Bärenreiter, Kassel, 1959.
Vitry, Philippe de
  Ars Contrapunctus, published in Coussemaker, *Scriptorum . . . ,*
    Vol. III.
Vogler, Abbé Georg Joseph
  Choral-System, Copenhagen, 1800.
Zarlino, Gioseffo
  Istitutioni harmoniche, Francesco Senese, Venice, 1558, 1562, 1573.

Index

154

F

Fa, 31, 39
  see also Mi contra fa
Fétis, xiv, 151
Fifth, 20, 71, 97, 109, 111, 112, 142
  successions of, see Successions
Fourth, 20
  augmented, see Tritone
  considered a dissonance, 20, 98, 142
  considered an imperfect consonance,
    20, 131, 142
  as nota cambiata, 51
  to be resolved to the fifth, 58
  to be resolved to the third, 56
  skip of, see Skips

G

Garlandia, vii, 150
Gluck, xii
Griesinger, xi, 150

H

Handel, x
Harmonic division, 20, 111, 141 ff.
Harmonic triad, 71 ff., 86, 95, 109, 123
Haydn, xi ff., 20, 133, 150, 151
Haydon, 150
Hexachords, 31, 35
Hidden fifths, see Successions
Hidden octaves, see Successions
Hindemith, xiv
Hummel, xiv

I

Imitation, 110
Imperfect consonances, see Consonances
Intervals, 20
  augmented, 27
  compound, 36, 110
  diminished, 27

J

Jeppesen, x, xiv, 35, 36, 41, 52, 65, 93,
  97, 150

L

Lang, xi
Ligatures (or syncopations, or ties, or
    suspensions), 55 ff., 65, 67, 87,
    94 ff., 127 ff., 136
  consonant, 55
  dissonant, 55 ff., 98
  interrupted, 62
Liszt, xiv

M

Magnus, xii
Mandyczewski, xiv
Manfredi, xv, 149
Mann, 149, 150
Martini, xii, 20, 22, 50, 92, 99, 130, 133,
  150
Mattheson, xv, 150
Mensural notation, 144
Meyerbeer, xiv
Mi, 31
  followed by fa, 74
  leading up, 39
  mi contra fa, 35, 46
  occurring in the bass, 73
Mizler, xv, 149
Modes, xi, xv, 28, 31, 33, 46
Monochord, 141, 143
Monotonia, see Sequences
Monteverdi, ix, 150
Moscheles, xiv
Motions, 20 ff.
  contrary, 21, 22
    to be employed as often as possible,
    27
  direct, 21
    see also Successions
  oblique, 21, 22, 29, 65, 106
    allowed with all progressions, 22
Mozart, L., xii